BEYOND
the
CURTAIN
1981–2014

BEYOND
the
CURTAIN
1981–2014

*Stories and reflections
on travelling in Eastern Europe*

DAVID BLAIR

THE CHOIR PRESS

To the memory of my late wife Valerie who stood by me in all the varied circumstances of these years.

Contents

꧁꧂

Acknowledgements

My deep gratitude to those who travelled with me; to those who travelled to assist in speaking, teaching, training; to those whose wisdom meant so much to me over the years, and not least to all who prayed for me.

In our Watford-based prayer group we met regularly with Rob and Dori Dawes, Elizabeth and Tony Harlow, Brian and Jean Hogg, Peter Kerr, Chris and Pam Lilley, Brian and Jackie Mee, Joy and Robert Simpson, Jack and Pat Watson, Peter Zimmermann and others who joined our prayer group from time to time.

Travellers included Jim Hartley, Peter Hyson, Denise Trotter, Tim Dawes, Tim Blair, Heather Keep, Alison Houghton-Kral, Keith Judson, Brian Sedgwick, Richard Wallis, Peter Graystone, Judith Merrill, Emlyn Williams, John Grayston, Cathie Smith, Geoff Ovens, Janet Morgan, Ruth and Bryan Nicholls, Alex Williams, Margaret Old and Claire-Lise de Benoit. The much-appreciated support and practical guidance from Karl Shafer, Danilo Gay, David Cohen, Ron Buckland, John Dean, Emmanuel Oladipo, Nigel Sylvester, Alan Martin, Peter Hoppler, Fritz Hoppler, Daniel Poujol, Jan Heitman, Franz Jenni and others was of great value as I sought to listen and learn from colleagues, mentors and friends.

And fellow workers (the first and early staff, volunteers, and council/board 'chairs' in the 'new' SU movements in Central and Eastern Europe): Lydia Trnkova, Brian Sedgwick, Jiri Lukl, Daniel and Janet Berkovic, Anica Kerep, Lazar Stojsic, Olga Dega, Melita Vidovic, Jan Tomczyk, Wojciech Muranty, Isa Has, Piotr Zaremba, Nelu Dan, Rodica Magdas, John Anderson, David and Valerie Hornsby, Bulcsú Széll, Beata Toth, Erzsebet Komlosi, Tamás Daxner, Gabor Keleti, Natalia Luptakova, Alena and Vlado Lachova, Stefan

Markus, Helen Parry, Blaga Popova, Michaela Petrova ... and to all my colleagues in the IFES movements in Europe ...

Much more recently I want to thank Brian and BLynn Bowen, Hilki and Denida and others who have lit the SU flame in Kosovo.

Finally: almost certainly I have missed out some important incidents, journeys and the names of people who were involved in different ways in building this work in Eastern Europe. My sources of information were incomplete in places. The account is necessarily incomplete. I have written what I now remember and am happy to leave it at that!

And my thanks to Hilary, my wife, who has been infinitely patient and generous with her time in advising me, discussing with me much of what I have written here and correcting many mistakes in the manuscript!

Introduction:
Winter 1983 – With the Skis Attached

―― ৶ ৹ ――

'Everything out!'

The stony-faced, determined Polish border guard left us with no options but to comply. My travelling companion looked at me apprehensively.

Alex and I had loaded the car with the most amazing variety of food, medicines and creature comforts. On reaching the Czech/Polish border after overnight stops in Central Germany and Kutná Hora, we had hit communist officialdom with a vengeance in a short but blunt exchange when we had tried in vain to make light of the fact that we were carrying an apparently innocuous letter in Polish to a Polish pastor. Or had it been a final order when my companion had tried to ward off any further enquiries about what we were doing coming late in the evening from Czechoslovakia in a car packed with a variety of food, airbeds, medicines, books and much else besides, with a pair of skis on the roof? No matter; the message was abundantly clear.

When we had meekly emptied the car and carried the contents, through the driving snow, to a small grey brick-built guard house a few metres away, we were questioned and the car was thoroughly searched. The search included taking the studded back panel off the driver's seat, with a Polish hand feeling round every little crevice – looking for illegal substances or illegal currency or worse. I never subsequently managed to get the panel fitted properly.

In the guard house, each item of luggage was scrupulously examined, papers and film strips taken away for photocopying, boxes emptied, and questions continued to be put to us, brusquely and without an ounce of humour or human feeling. What did they intend to do with the luggage? Would they send us back to Czecho-slovakia, with or without our bananas and our camp beds? I silently thought back to the events of thirty minutes earlier, when we had left Czechoslovakia with a wan smile from a female border guard, who had spoken excellent English and had accepted a Christian booklet from our varied stock of literature. If we met her again, surely she would understand with her kind and almost friendly farewell.

We waited patiently for the gruffly spoken Poles to complete their search and give us their verdict, or our sentence! With an almost dismissive wave of the hand, they indicated that we could take our luggage, now strewn on their chipped brown-topped tables, and proceed to enter Poland. This 'interrogation' was our longest at any border, around four hours. It took us some time to repack, but we were relieved and thankful to God that this epic car trip from the White Cliffs of Dover to Poland was not in vain. Much more was yet to happen ...

*

I am writing this story more than thirty years on. I have had time to pray and to reflect; to gather together records of my travels during the years of restriction and discrimination facing many of our sisters and brothers in Christ, and in the subsequent years of freedom and democracy for the countries of Central and Eastern Europe. Mary Sarotte (in *1989: The Struggle to Create Post-Cold War Europe*) writes: 'On November 9, 1989, the Berlin Wall opened and the world changed.'[1] This seismic, historic event was perhaps the unexpected culmination of forty repressive years when these countries were bound together, without popular consent, by the Warsaw Pact, imposed by their Soviet masters.

But that part of my personal story about which I am writing began thirty-five years ago, in the ice-cold January of 1981, when I

---

[1] Mary Sarotte. *1989: The Struggle to Create Post-Cold War Europe*. Woodstock: Princeton University Press, 2009

took my first intrepid journey through the 'Iron Curtain'. This memorable description was spoken by Winston Churchill in his post-war speech of 5th March 1946 when he famously declared: 'From Stettin in the Baltic to Trieste in the Adriatic an iron curtain has descended across the continent. Behind that line lie all the capitals of the ancient states of Central and Eastern Europe. Warsaw, Berlin, Prague, Vienna, Budapest, Belgrade, Bucharest and Sofia; all these famous cities and the populations around them lie in what I must call the Soviet sphere, and all are subject, in one form or another, not only to Soviet influence but to a very high and in some cases increasing measure of control from Moscow.'[2]

It is now almost one hundred years since the Bolsheviks established the world's first communist regime, encompassing one sixth of the globe. On the 23rd February 1917, marking International Women's Day and an acute bread shortage, thousands of female textile workers and housewives took to the streets of the Russian capital (Petrograd – St Petersburg), launching a revolution lasting over seventy years and a consequence of which was the forty years of Soviet dominance in the countries of Eastern Europe following the end of World War II. Yet all that 'brief history' pales into insignificance against the background of the greater and more radical revolution of love launched by the crucified Messiah, Jesus of Nazareth, 2,000 years before, the flames of which were never extinguished even in the harshest of times in the Soviet empire, when persecution, accusation and dehumanisation challenged the rights and the presence of communities of Christian believers. All this bore witness to the power of the Cross and the Resurrection in the dying and rising again of the Church of Jesus Christ in the Soviet Union and in its satellites in Central and Eastern Europe.

Following my first visit to Eastern Europe, the thought that I would be travelling through and to these cities recalled by Winston

---

[2] Klaus Dodds. *Geopolitics: A Very Short Introduction*. Oxford: Oxford University Press, 2007

Churchill was well beyond my normal expectations and anticipations. My book sets out to chart some personal stories: journeys, encounters with glum, iron-fisted border guards and more friendly fellow travellers, but above all meeting with and working alongside wonderful, gracious people, many of whom had withstood the totalitarian forces behind that hideous curtain and had done so in the belief that the God they worshipped was the supreme ruler of the universe and the compassionate Father who would draw many to Himself.

This is a personal story, written to encourage and inform my family – my children: Anastasia, Andrew, Tim and Liz, and my grandchildren: Sarah, Ben, Ashley, Aimée, Ellie and Daniel. They have been wonderfully supportive over the years when my life circumstances have changed and now, as I grow into and discover what it means to live in a lower register. But I would also like to share the story with others who have an interest in Eastern Europe, including a number who supported me in the years of travel and discovery.

From the beginning, my late wife Valerie stood with me; she offered practical wisdom, supportive love and a down-to-earth prayerful life. In all my sometimes crazy travel plans, my dreams, my expectations, she shared in the disappointments, of which there were more than a few, as well as the joys – abundant and enduring, as we together witnessed the faith and depth of the lives of many Christians and their response to new ideas and new ways of bringing people the experience and ethos of Scripture Union and the International Fellowship of Evangelical Students (IFES), for whom I worked.

I also want to pay tribute to the many who worked with me and prayed for me (see acknowledgements at the beginning of the book).

During the time I was travelling to Eastern Europe, until retirement in 1998, I was a Scripture Union staff member, based in England, seconded from 1990 to the European Region of Scripture Union, but from 1986 I had been seconded as a part-time high schools consultant in the European IFES staff team. Much that I have written relates to the development of SU movements in Central and Eastern Europe, but I include some stories of activities, events and meeting people whose focus was the establishing or strengthening of a high schools ministry throughout the continent of Europe. These two complementary roles dovetailed well. Occasionally, questions were (rightly and sensitively) raised as to the complexities of a dual role. In practical 'everyday' terms, I found it enormously enriching to work with two Christian movements that had similar goals and compatible philosophies of ministry.

Finally in this introduction, I want to apologise in advance for the inevitability of any (I hope) minor errors of fact or interpretation, and maybe a few (not too glaring?) omissions. Much of what I have written has been crafted from personal memory. I want to thank those who have jogged my memory and provided me with valuable resources and illustrations. I hope that you will enjoy the read!

Through the Curtain in 1981

———❧❧———

I first travelled alone to Poland in January 1981, to meet and work with Polish Christians in leading a children's camp in the remote border hills in the south-west of the country. Three years earlier the white smoke had come out of the Vatican chimney and the Cardinal of Krakow had become Pope John Paul II. John Paul II's elevation could be said to be at the root of the rise of the anti-communist Solidarity movement, led by the charismatic figure of Lech Wałęsa. Fears of instability in this most populous of the Eastern European satellites brought swift and secret deals – were KGB agents behind the plot to assassinate the Pope?

At the time, I was blissfully unaware of these larger political machinations. Nevertheless, some troubling questions were buzzing around in my head as the train from Frankfurt sped towards the East German border around midnight on that late January night. What might I expect to find? How should I prepare? Should I be carrying the twelve copies of a basic daily Bible reading guide which had been translated into Polish? What if the border guards searched my luggage? What would they make of my SU soundstrips (now somewhat dated 'media resources' which consisted of filmstrips with a taped commentary)? Actually, when the Polish border guards found them and examined them, they were highly amused at the cartoon artwork; no question of them confiscating either the filmstrips or me. They handed them back to me without an English word, only a broad grin, and the accompanying passengers in the train looked on in amazement.

In Frankfurt earlier that day, I had been met by Jon, the no-nonsense IFES co-ordinator in Central Europe, who quizzed me, making sure that I knew exactly why I was going to Poland and that

God was in it! 'If he's not, then catch the next plane back to London.' Jon's words were firm and clear. He had a long history of working behind the Iron Curtain and had had many brushes with official-dom at the borders and elsewhere. He had even swallowed his address list in one of the more restricted countries, to avoid compro-mising his Eastern European friends on the list.

At twelve noon the next day, the train pulled into Jelenia Góra, a sizeable city in industrial south-west Poland, where the flags were flying (for Solidarity, the Polish workers' movement for change and renewal) and where I was met by Witek Zachanowicz and his welcoming Polish family. But before we could leave the station for their home, I had to send a telegram to Valerie. This had not been my idea, but Jon had asked me to send a 'signal' via a telegram to Valerie that it was 'safe' for him to take a western-registered vehicle to a student camp which he was helping to run in Poland in the week following my visit. Some years later (in 1995) my wife, Valerie, speaking at an SU supporters' meeting in Bury St Edmunds, said:

> Fourteen years ago, coinciding with the rise of the Solidarity movement, David (my husband) made his first visit to Poland in Eastern Europe. As far as I was concerned it seemed as risky as a trip to the North Pole! His brother strongly advised him not to go, but of course, as those of you who know David might expect, he went! I was told that I would be unlikely to hear from him during the fortnight he was away – telephone systems in Poland at that time were not quite up to BT standard ... *but* I did receive a telegram from him. The wording was fairly inconsequential but great to have. However a few days later I had a mysterious phone call asking if I had heard from David. When I replied in the affirmative, the caller asked me to read the telegram to him. Apparently it was a pre-arranged coded message, but I only learnt about that after David's return. I really felt that I had been caught up in an East/West espionage incident. But it was as a result of that visit that David's love of Eastern Europe grew and his desire to help the Christians there in whatever way he could.

7

On his part, Witek was more than amused as he couldn't see there would be any problem with bringing a western vehicle. In reality, his more relaxed response was a reflection of the greater freedom in Poland than was normal in most of the other Warsaw Pact countries of Eastern Europe.

Yet there were pressures amidst politics. In her book *Light and Life: Renewal in Poland* Grazyna Sikorska writes about the 'Oasis' retreats. In the summer of 1981, 45,000 young people applied to attend retreats, before food rationing was introduced and Oasis, treated as 'illegal' camps by the authorities, could not buy food. Father Franciszek Blachnicki immediately appealed to the west for help, and soon eleven trucks, each carrying twenty tons of food, arrived in Poland. The 'Light-Life' movement, cradled in the early 1950s, was a Catholic renewal/charismatic movement for young people. Blachnicki, the founder, had organised the first retreat at the height of Stalinist terror and, when the secret police and their informants were at their most vigilant, with 200 altar boys meeting in the woods to escape the attention of security police. By the mid-1970s, Campus Crusade for Christ (Agape) and Youth with a Mission (YWAM) were working in close co-operation with Light-Life, although Polish Protestants seem to have kept their distance. Nevertheless this was a significant 'revival movement' in Poland over thirty years or more and through it many came to a personal faith in Christ. Blachnicki died in 1987, but the movement has taken root in a number of countries, including the UK.

Witek explained to me as best he could the nature of the children's and youth camp and what might be expected of me. His English was near perfect; the uncertainties were solely related to the organising of the camp – the programme planning would be accomplished mostly after the camp began!

On the following day (Sunday), starting well before daylight at 5.10am, we travelled by two slow trains (one diesel, one steam) and an even slower bus to Bielice, a tiny village only a few kilometres from the Czech border. The final bus journey from Kłodzko to our destination saw a border guard join us to check papers. My presence could have aroused suspicion; as a foreigner, what was I doing in such a sensitive border region? Sitting alongside Witek I remained silent, as the guard walked impassively and slowly to the back of the bus, with only a cursory glance at our documents.

The camp started the same day. Soon after arrival and lunch, we held our first meeting, Witek translating for me; but Witek, who was a secondary school teacher, set off before dusk, on the long and slow journey back to his wife Eva and their two children. He was required to teach the following week; he had expected to be free to translate for me for the week, but at remarkably short notice his school mid-term break had been changed. I was left at the campsite with about twelve to fifteen young people, mostly in their mid-to-late teens, and a Christian farmer and his wife, neither of whom could speak English – nor were any of the teenagers confident English speakers, although one could speak and understand more English than the others. Of course, I was the least equipped, speaking not one word of Polish other than the standard greeting 'dzień dobry'.

The young people all decided that evening that we would hold another meeting and that I would speak! My hurried 'game plan' included showing a Scripture Union soundstrip on Creation. I thought this would be just possible as the words on the script were simply Bible verses from Genesis 1 and Psalm 104. Two of the teenagers agreed to read the appropriate verses (in Polish, of course) where the tape would have been playing them; the only problem was how to prompt them to 'come in' at the right moment. We did some hurried rehearsals, showed the filmstrip – then they had a protracted discussion about it in Polish. It seemed to produce a response ...

It had to get better. *I'm here for a week, at least, before Witek returns to take me elsewhere in Poland,* I mused silently.

On the following day, the Baptist pastor Rev. Alex Kircun arrived. His English was well polished, and we sat down and planned the programme – he would give some lectures on problems that the young people would face at school concerning the reliability of the

The farmhouse where many Christian camps were run over the years before ('in secret') and after 1989

gospels; I would give a series of talks on what being a Christian was about in a 'secular' environment. Alex Kircun was none other than the son of Alex Kircun senior, the Polish pastor from Warsaw who had met John and Marion Laird sixteen years earlier, and who had been involved in the distribution of the 'imported' SU Bible reading cards, printed in London. A continuing part of God's plan for Scripture Union in Poland?

*

Looking back, Scripture Union's presence in Poland had been there for many years. Before World War II, the reading card, Bible reading notes and magazines were printed in a variety of Slavic languages. I had found snippets of information about work in some of the Central European countries in SU England's archives, but these were teasingly few. In 1934, when the SU badge was 6d and when you could purchase a portable organ (for use at beach missions and other events) for £6/15/-, a note in the CSSM magazine spoke of

Pastor Gotze of Warsaw who wrote, 'The Lord is blessing the distribution of the Scripture Union cards in Poland ... people of the Orthodox church are reading the Bible through the help of these cards ... the priest is so interested that he sent us a small gift and wrote the following: "For the distribution of Scripture Union Cards for daily Bible reading".'

John Laird led the SU movement in England and Wales from 1944 to 1968, and visited Poland in 1965. He wrote in his subsequent report:

We were attending the week-night meeting of a church in Warsaw. About 80 church members were present. I had given a message and spoken about SU, holding in my hand a Polish SU Reading card. Towards the end of the meeting the choir sang for the second time, and I noticed above their heads some words in Polish with the reference Isaiah 26:19 'O dwellers in the dust awake and sing for joy'.

These words were movingly appropriate to all that we saw and heard during our four days in Warsaw. We realised that many of those present had indeed been 'children of the dust'. During the German occupation, Warsaw was the centre of the resistance movement, and of the struggle against the Nazis. On the 1st of August 1944, the Warsaw Rising broke out. It lasted 63 days and during that time no less than 200,000 perished. After capitulation by the brave resistance fighters, the city was evacuated, and the Nazis set about the planned demolition; astonishingly 87% of buildings, including bridges, hospitals, universities, museums and over 900 historic buildings, were destroyed either in part or completely devastated. During the whole occupation of Warsaw, 750,000 inhabitants met their death. After the war, in a great wave of patriotism, the city was restored. A special tax was levied, many worked in the ruins for little or no pay, many churches and ancient buildings were restored in exact replicas and look today almost precisely as they did before the destruction. Many new buildings were erected. Among these, close to the heart of the city, there is a new Baptist church. The land on which it stands was the scene of many brutal executions. Its pastor, who for many years has been president of the

Baptist Union of Poland, is also our Scripture Union representative. He told us that his church was built on the foundation of blood and bone. On this soil of human suffering and tragedy now flourishes a living church. Modern in style, it was designed by two architects, one a Roman Catholic and the other a Protestant, and when it was opened there were representatives of all the major denominations.

It is evident that Scripture Union reading cards are much appreciated in many churches. Their mode of distribution is unusual. They are handed round the congregation on the collection plate on the first Sunday of the year. Undoubtedly there is scope for a greatly increased SU ministry in Poland, not only for cards, but for notes. This was made clear to us by a number of church leaders including a representative of the Polish Bible Society. Of all countries in Eastern Europe, Poland enjoys the greatest measure of independence and liberty, both politically and religiously. The circulation of the scriptures is steadily increasing and a modern translation of the whole Bible will be published next year. This would be an ideal opportunity to give a new impetus to Scripture Union, and to build on the goodwill which has already been established by a fairly wide distribution of SU Cards over many years. Poland is the obvious centre from which Christian influences can spread to other countries in Eastern Europe. Careful plans would have to be made, including a visit next year, and some financial help would be necessary. Should funds become available this would undoubtedly be an excellent investment for the extension of the kingdom of God in very needy areas.

During that visit, John Laird visited a theological college with four students, where they were offered Polish Bibles and encouragement about the work of Scripture Union. In 1967 John returned to Poland when he not only visited a number of churches throughout the country, but spoke at an inter-confessional conference about the SU Bible reading 'method' and the use of the reading card. John had gained wide acceptance amongst a variety of churches, perhaps because he came from outside the country and was seen to be free from the internal divisions and the curious sense of suspicion that existed between denominations. Later Mr Wojnar, a Polish pastor, travelled round the country promoting Scripture Union. These were the strong roots that enabled us to begin again in the eighties.

*

The camp had finished; many young people returned home with their faith strengthened and a few had encountered Jesus for the first time in their lives. On the final Saturday, Witek returned and we travelled together back to Wrocław, a large city in Lower Silesia. Prior to World War II, Wrocław, known as Breslau, was part of the Third Reich. In 1933, 200,000 of its citizens had voted for Hitler's party in the elections. From that moment on, the Nazis strengthened their hold over the city, launching a campaign of terror. Synagogues were burnt to the ground on Kristallnacht – 9th November 1938 – and the guillotine at Kleczkowska prison saw plenty of action, with the decapitated bodies of political prisoners donated to Breslau/ Wrocław's medical schools. The city became part of Poland under the terms of the Potsdam Conference after the Second World War, and when only a tiny fraction of the population was German.

The Second Baptist church was an old building with a large and thriving congregation and where, on the following day (Sunday), clad in an ill-fitting borrowed jacket taken hurriedly out of a cavernous wardrobe in the pastor's flat adjacent to the church, I was invited to preach. Witek was a flawless translator, translating fluently without my having to make a break. I asked him if he translated everything that visiting preachers spoke. He said, 'No – not even you!' and pointed out that I had in my sermon referred to the children's and young people's camp in the remote farmhouse in Bielice; he had omitted this because, as he said, he could never tell whether a security agent was spying in the church that morning. But also, in hushed tones, he told me that sometimes, and especially if the western visitor was preaching an 'over-long' sermon or was saying something he didn't agree with, he simply omitted things!

On that second Sunday evening, after standing in a long queue at Wrocław's rather too functional and dull-looking rail station, waiting to purchase rail tickets, we travelled north to Gdańsk and Gdynia. While I was talking to Witek in the slow-moving queue, he whispered in a mild caution that we should change the subject of our conversation as the person behind seemed to be paying undue attention to what we had been talking about – Witek assumed that he might be a member of the Polish KGB! Witek had previously been 'tracked' by a security agent; he was a member of Solidarity, and security people were aware of that and regularly checked on his movements and his activities. So Poland, although freer than other countries in the eastern 'bloc', was not entirely free from the overall constricts of a communist regime.

We arrived in Gdynia – adjacent to Gdańsk/Danzig, one of the ports of the Hanseatic League in mediaeval times – early the following morning, for a three-day visit. We first went to the hospital where Ela, Witek's sister, worked as a doctor, and with the key to her flat in Witek's pocket, we showered and ate a welcome breakfast.

After an unsuccessful visit to the shops to buy cheese, we witnessed something of the normal daily life: a long queue. The rumour was that washing machines would soon be available to purchase, and people were waiting patiently and anxiously to place an order for this vital piece of domestic equipment – delivery of which was anticipated in six months. Neither was there any meat on the lunch menu in the otherwise attractive 'Polonia' restaurant; we settled for fish and chips washed down with Pepsi.

During our time in Gdańsk and Gdynia we led some meetings about Bible reading, evangelism and what was happening in SU worldwide. The hunger to know what God was doing in the world outside the strict confines of Poland was quite remarkable and humbling. Before we had left Wrocław for the overnight trip to Gdańsk and Gdynia, I had purchased a small and simple slide/filmstrip projector, operated from my knees. It cost the equivalent of £7 in Polish currency. On my return home, some of my English Scripture Union colleagues looked at the tiny machine with a measure of disdain, and pronounced it a toy! But it was effective in conveying, visually, the immense diversity of SU worldwide, as we showed a number of SU soundstrips with the commentaries translated superbly by Witek. He and I had spent one morning in Gdańsk sitting in the modest but well-furnished British Council suite, drinking coffee and planning the best way to show the sound-strips.

Later that week, we travelled back to Jelenia Góra on another tiring all-night train journey. During the remainder of my days in the country we visited several small mid-week congregations in south-west Poland, where I had further opportunities to illustrate and talk about the work of SU and to challenge Christian believers about the vital importance of daily Bible reading.

Fifteen days after I arrived in Poland, I took the same route back to Frankfurt; the compartment was full of friendly Polish young people, some of whom spoke English. I slept a little on a harsh top-level couchette and, before catching the flight back to the UK, ate a fine breakfast in a Frankfurt restaurant the following morning.

At the Heart of a Crumbling Empire

————— ℰ ℐ —————

In the late eighties and early nineties, the political, cultural and religious scene in Eastern Europe was changing dramatically and fundamentally. Mikhail Gorbachev, the chief architect of perestroika and glasnost, was heralding a new age of freedom and democracy in both the Soviet Union and its Eastern European satellite states. For millions, there was restlessness, resentment, anger, anxiety. 'The sixteen year wait for a car and the 25 year wait for a telephone were no longer tolerable.' [1]

Almost ten years to the day after my first intrepid journey into Poland, on an early morning in the February of 1991, I stood calmly waiting in the check-in queue at Tallinn airport. Outside, it was seasonally cold and white. But this was no bizarre micro-climate; the winter freeze covering the northern half of the former Soviet Union, of which Tallinn stood at the western edge, was all-embracing in its icy grip. Unsurprisingly, after checking in my over-weighted baggage, I was informed solemnly that the incoming flight from Moscow to Tallinn was delayed because of heavy snow in the Russian capital. How late? No one seemed to know or even care. The subsequent announcement had an ominous ring of finality about it. The flight was cancelled.

I had spent the previous ten days in the Soviet Union, in Moscow, St Petersburg and Tallinn, seeking to introduce Scripture Union and the opportunities for Christian ministry in high schools. A few months before this, in October 1990, I had begun what would be my longest visit to Eastern Europe. The three weeks would take me first

---

[1] Mary Sarotte. *1989: The Struggle to Create Post-Cold War Europe*. Woodstock: Princeton University Press, 2009

to Russia and Estonia, followed by a week in Romania, and finally a week back in Moscow. I travelled with Pete Lowman (who was an IFES pioneer in these early days of post-communist freedoms) for the first time to Moscow, St Petersburg and Tallinn where I had many opportunities, alongside more than a few extraordinary experiences.

In Moscow, Pete and I attended the first ever Moscow-based Lausanne Congress. Fifteen hundred delegates, mostly Russian, met for five days of talks, discussions, seminars, exhibitions. Only a few weeks before we had left London, en route to Estonia, Moscow and St Petersburg, we had been told that any resources we took for distribution or display at the Congress had to be in Russian. In answer to prayer, I found Anna, who not only translated some shortened versions of our Bible reading notes but came with us to help with translation on the floor of the giant exhibition hall. I had also sent to the Congress separately not only quantities of these translated and hastily printed materials, but additionally copies of some SU soundstrips with translated commentaries. These arrived late and after the conference was well under way. So, with nothing to show on the empty table allocated to us other than photographs of Scripture Union activities, we simply prayed that these resources would arrive before the end of the conference – and they did! And when we began to put them out, we found ourselves swamped by many Russian pastors and others representing their own communities, who were hungry for materials and resources.

This was only a beginning, and later Danilo Gay from Switzerland – Danilo was again a pioneer and had worked with SU in Zaire and Canada for a number of years before he sensed the call of God to start afresh in the Soviet Bloc – took over the development of SU work in Russia and its satellites. Today, through the faithfulness and wisdom of Danilo Gay and Michael Rowe, there are a number of flourishing SU movements in these same former Soviet states, run effectively by people such as Grigori Stupak, Oksana Khimich, Andrei Cherniak, Vera Zhuravleva, Dimitri Bazarov and others – all national staff and leaders of movements which took root in the early and mid-nineties.

On the first day of my visit in 1990, we had travelled from Moscow to Estonia. Arriving in Tallinn late in the evening, I phoned Leho, a seventeen-year-old schoolboy, whose name I had been given through Pete Lowman. 'Yes,' he said, 'please come to my school at 7.15 in the morning. We can meet the Head and then you will be able to take some lessons.'

Shortly after arriving, I found myself in a class of senior pupils studying 'suffering' and I talked about CS Lewis and 'the problem of pain'. I suppose most of these young people had never met an English person before and certainly not in their classroom. Later in the week, I had opportunities in 'School 54' to speak to several classes of younger children. In one class, the teacher – a Christian – had asked the children to cut out shapes and put a Bible verse on them. They loved being asked by their teacher to present these to me at the end of the lesson.

We travelled to Tartu, where again I was free to take classes. All this was an introduction to exploring the possibilities for a schools ministry in Estonia.

Within four months I travelled again, in February 1991, to Moscow, St Petersburg and Estonia. At the time, it was a disappointing and quite lonely visit, with little to encourage me about the possibilities of Scripture Union taking root in the vast Soviet empire.

My two days in Moscow found me donning a new Russian hat. When my host saw me arriving in British woolly headgear, she rushed back to her flat to find me a much warmer fur-covered beauty! We met briefly with a representative of the Russian Bible Society. We talked about options for introducing Scripture Union in Moscow, but without any obvious or immediate plans or responses.

In St Petersburg, I spent some hours waiting for the telephone to ring and some new contacts to be firmed up. Without the help and friendship of a Jewish man, whom I had met in Bucharest airport some months earlier and whose telephone number I had remembered to bring with me, I might have been stranded in a cold, remote hotel on the outskirts of the city for the weekend. Yet Ivan the Jew returned early from his planned weekend with the family and, arriving in his Lada, he took me to the Baptist church on Sunday morning where I was to meet one of the leaders, as the Baptist baboushkas, emerging from the lengthy morning service, snaked down in a long line from the hill where the church was situated. I spoke briefly at an after-church meeting to a few Sunday school teachers, who seemed more than anxious to get back home! There had been few opportunities to meet church leaders and others, and to explore options for beginning a high schools ministry.

From St Petersburg I flew to Tallinn in Estonia, for a more encouraging few days, meeting up with Leho Paldre and others. From that encounter came a visit of an Estonian choir to England in October of the following year, when we travelled the length and breadth of the UK – as far north as Aberdeen and as far south as Sevenoaks, with eight concerts in as many days. We were able to use this opportunity to share news about the work in Eastern Europe with a much wider audience.

Sometime after I had returned to the UK, it was agreed that my brief for all the former communist regimes was too demanding. Danilo Gay from Switzerland and Michael Rowe would step into taking responsibility for the 'Federation of Soviet Republics' (FSR).

At the end of those few days in Tallinn, in that snowy winter of 1991, I stood feeling helpless in Tallinn's unfriendly airport, asking myself, *How do I cope with a cancelled flight?* In the Soviet Union, Intourist, the state agency for travelling everywhere and anywhere under careful supervision, was still very much in control, and so their black-leather-coated representative confidently but coldly predicted, when I enquired about how I would get to Moscow, that I would be offered first-class train travel from Tallinn to arrive in Moscow the following morning. Meanwhile I would be taken back to my Tallinn hotel for the day, and then to the rail station to catch the night train.

Finally reunited with my luggage (which, on the first attempt to check in, had been thrown on the belt and had disappeared into what looked like a cavernous storage building, and which I rescued with the help of the airport manager), I queued up again at the check-in having discovered that, after all, my flight to Moscow was now back on – due to leave around three hours later than scheduled. I would have about thirty minutes to get from Moscow's national airport to the international terminal. Yet the timing was perfect and at around 6pm we departed for London on a comfortable, half-empty British Airways jumbo. I sat back, relaxed, and thanked the Lord for getting me this far; nor was I ungrateful for everything that was British. I ate a hearty supper. But little did I realise what lay ahead.

As we circled Heathrow three and a half hours later – 6.30pm GMT – the pilot laconically announced that Heathrow was being subjected to a blizzard; traffic was held up on the M25 and rail services were severely disrupted. Never mind; I knew that Valerie would not fail me – she would be there waiting faithfully for me to emerge from the baggage collection point and into the arrivals hall, to greet me lovingly, and then skilfully to drive me home through blizzard and ice! How foolish of me to think that my wife was superhuman. In the event, Valerie was not there to greet me, and when I got through on the coin box phone, she, in some distress, told me that it was impossible for her to come; nor could she persuade a single taxi driver in Watford to risk life and limb in order to pick me up at Terminal 2.

It took two long and frustrating hours to reach Euston station, only to discover that there was one and only one train departing for Watford before midnight. Around 11.30pm we left Euston, four and a half hours after I had landed at Heathrow (much longer than flying from Moscow to London).

Watford Junction was exceedingly white. I staggered down to the forecourt a few minutes after midnight, to face an empty taxi rank and a one-mile walk home, dragging cases (without wheels) behind me. As I approached the roundabout at the end of St Albans Road, I caught sight of two seemingly lonely figures moving hesitantly towards me, through the deepening snow. None other than Valerie and our lodger! She had persuaded him to come with her to meet me. Being the determined woman she was, she had calculated with some precision the exact time when I would be walking home from the station. The lodger picked up the bags and within ten minutes I stepped over the threshold of my most welcome home.

The next morning, I did not rise too early. But nevertheless we thanked the Lord for safety and for giving me a sense of proportion, humour and peace in all the changes of that one day. And for the tiny seeds planted in Tallinn, St Petersburg and Moscow.

Poland in the Eighties:
Seeing Lives Changed

———— e. ————

These visits, to Poland in 1981 and to the former Soviet Union ten years later, were both mindblowing but greatly humbling experiences. They helped shape my thinking and living, acutely aware that I had received much more than I could ever give; that I had encountered people whose lives greatly challenged mine; that my methods and strategies for developing a high schools ministry or a Scripture Union movement might require some radical recasting.

Through the eighties I travelled several times to Poland; not, of course, in 1982 when martial law had been declared and when it was all but impossible for foreigners to obtain visas during that tense period of Poland's history. On occasion I journeyed by car but always with a companion. In 1983 and 1984 I was accompanied by the redoubtable Alex Williams (for his story of emerging student ministry in Eastern Europe see his book *Holy Spy*). Alex had studied ceramics as a postgraduate at Krakow University during the seventies and had taken timely opportunities of working closely with Christian students. God had blessed that work. Alex was a skilled linguist, an unbounded enthusiast and greatly gifted in developing trustful friendships on behalf of Jesus!

In the winter of 1983 (as I wrote in the introduction), heading for Poland via Germany, Pilsen and Kutná Hora in Bohemia, the green Alpine Talbot hatch had left Watford almost full with all kinds of supplies for the journey and the destination. I hadn't bargained for Alex's enthusiasm and optimism as we loaded blankets, mattresses, fresh vegetables and a further assortment of 'necessary' supplies before finally calling in at the local supermarket in rural Sussex for a wide range of perishables and consumables, to add weight to the already overloaded vehicle. On top were skis, a move on our part designed to convince the ever-suspicious border guards in Eastern Europe that we were only humble tourists heading for the cheaper slopes!

Following our four or five hour 'delay' at the Czech/Polish border when the car was all but emptied under the prying eyes of the Polish border guards, we made our way to the nearest village where we found a basic hostel. Knocking up the proprietor at 1.30 in the morning was stock in trade, it seemed, for Alex, a seasoned veteran of East European travel. We slept well and arrived at the campsite in Bielice the following morning. The facilities in the farmhouse had improved since I had first visited two years before (martial law had been introduced in December of 1981 and the winter of 1981/2 was no-go for westerners in Poland). We ate a hearty brunch, following which Alex brought in all the goods we had transported from England for the camp and began cooking some of the food!

We had been invited to assist in children's and young people's camps. We saw some real answers to prayer as Christian young people brought their non-Christian friends to these winter camps. One such was Nuisia (the younger sister of Witek), who brought her school-friend Marzena. Nuisia herself had established a small prayer and Bible study group meeting daily at (or, in the warmer and drier days, outside) school in the mornings as early as 7.15am. Nuisia wrote:

> I was talking to one of my classmates about the gospel. At that time she seemed to show little enthusiasm or interest in the things of God. So how surprised I was when a few days later, she expressed a desire to take part in our Christian camp at Bielice. This stirred up a curiosity, but also the opposition of predominantly Catholic class-mates ...[1]

---

[1] Alex Williams. *Holy Spy*. Harmat/Christian Focus, 2003

Marzena was curious and wanted to come with others. Her own family background was unhappy; on her first visit to Bielice she went back feeling angry and embittered, having observed a small Christian family (the local farmer who lived in the house where the camp was held) living out the Christian life that she knew nothing about. Yet she returned again after some months only to see the same family still living together in harmony. She could not understand it, but went home and simply began to read her Bible; for almost the whole night, she sat up and read and read, and as dawn broke, she knelt and committed her life to Jesus. In the early nineties Marzena became a key translator in the work of an English language school and theological school based at the Baptist church in Wrocław.

Nuisia wrote, following the winter camp:

> Over the next few months, God touched the hearts of three more girls in our class. Such a sudden flow of conversions naturally made not only the parents but also the teachers worry about these 'poisonous trends' … Later the Lord gave us opportunities to witness to our teachers; one of them, the Headmaster and a <u>real</u> communist (there were never very many of them in Poland!), engaged us in long debates about Christianity. He and his family even came to one of our camps in the mountains, and though he did not confess Christ at that time, I believe the seed of God's word was sown in his heart and that one day he will be called into God's kingdom.[2]

During our two weeks in Poland in '83, we were involved in the camps in two very different locations, both with very limited 'personal facilities' – the second week was in the town of Cieplice where we 'camped' in the Lutheran church parish hall. There was a surprising degree of freedom in witnessing for Christ in the public square. On Saturday afternoon we conducted an open-air meeting with songs and testimonies. Janos, a young man who was very

---

[2] Alex Williams. *Holy Spy*. Harmat/Christian Focus, 2003

Students meeting at camp in Bielice. Tomek (left) became the SU staff worker in 1996. Nuisia is second from the right

much on the edge of faith in 1981 when he came to Bielice and returned home early with his girlfriend who was not yet a Christian, was there at the camp in 1983 with a renewed faith in Christ! He had never driven a 'western' car before. We went out into the forest, where I handed over the steering wheel; he skidded down an icy road at speed, but amazingly negotiated the bends and the snow.

At the end of the second week of camps in 1983, we pointed the faithful Alpine Talbot westwards for the long journey home to the UK. Our first stop was Zgorzelec, marking the border with East Germany. Arriving late, we knocked on the door of a house where, we had been told before we left Cieplice, there was a Christian family. They welcomed us, fed us and moved their whole family into one room so that we might sleep in the other.

Early the following chilly morning, we set off to travel back across Europe. Alex was widely experienced in negotiating roads and rail, criss-crossing the continent. But before we departed Poland, I just had to take a photograph of a massive Polish steam train. As soon as I had taken the picture, one of our Polish companions tersely informed me that it was illegal to photograph public transport in Poland and I could have been arrested!

We drove on via the old Hitler-era motorway to Dresden, a grey and damaged city of historic significance still marred by the scars of the Second World War. We sat on hard seats in a proletarian restaurant for a basic but welcome lunch, and, after a lightning visit to the Zwinger Museum to view the Meissen porcelain treasures, we set off for Suhl, a spa town deep in the Thuringian forest.

As the light faded on the snow-covered hills shrouded with wandering mist, dim street lamps lit the main thoroughfare of Suhl; from the lamps hung large banners proclaiming (in German) 'Karl Marx lives in us and in our works'. We stayed overnight in the local tourist hotel, adjacent to the main square. Words of little consequence were exchanged between us, since Alex adjudged that, being adjacent to the local police station, the room might well be bugged!

Winter 1983: Young people at the Camp in Cieplice

Winter 1983: A detachment of the Red Army on a visit to the Meissen treasures

The following morning, Monday – a day on which I was determined to reach home – we drove first to Eisenach, visiting the Wartburg Castle, where the room in which Martin Luther had translated the New Testament was sadly closed. The bleak notice indicated that the room was temporarily closed for repairs 'in preparation for the 500th anniversary celebrations' of Luther's birth. Alex bought a dull-looking book. I was even less competent in understanding and reading German then than I am now, so Alex studied the contents of the book while I drove. I asked him if it was interesting and enlightening. 'Well,' he replied, 'of course. In this official biography of Martin Luther, he is described as the great early socialist!'

Soon then to the border, the iron curtain across Europe. It was a border crossing where a number of fleeing East Germans had met their end, attempting to jump barriers in a trace of bullets. Once through into West Germany, Alex pressed me to telephone Karl Schafer, SU's European regional secretary, to arrange to go to Marienheide and regale him with our Polish exploits. I was much less enthusiastic about that idea and was relieved when our Scripture Union colleagues at Marienheide indicated that Karl was out of town! It wasn't that I didn't wish to meet Karl, always a gracious, kind and encouraging person. I just wanted to get home and I could more easily send a written account to him of our Polish exploits.

Driving relentlessly towards Ostend, we reached the Belgian port just after midnight and took the next ferry for a 2am departure. There were no more than twelve passengers on the massive cross-channel boat. Alex settled down, enthusiastically tucking into his remaining dried rations. I just wanted to sleep.

The snow was deepening by the minute, as we cautiously made our way down the hill through Folkestone and finally to Newick by daylight. Alex was home and gently persuaded me to eat a 'real' breakfast. I consumed it swiftly and set out for Watford.

I felt burnt out at the end of this second and exhausting visit to Poland and longed to be back with my family again, in the safety and security of our home. Yet for all that, there was something about Alex's infectious enthusiasm which stuck with me and reinforced the call of God on my life, for that time.

The following year (1984), I returned to Poland with Alex to assist with a teenage and student camp, again in the remote Bielice village. The farm building as a Christian campsite had further developed its facilities – dormitories had been constructed on the upper floor. We had travelled on this occasion by borrowed car from Heilbronn in Germany. Having taken a flight from Heathrow to Frankfurt we had significantly less luggage and food supplies.

Driving again across Czechoslovakia, we took an alternative route through Prague, where we stopped briefly to visit Lydia Trnkova and her sister Marta and their families. Marta asked us gently but firmly not to speak as we descended the stairs when we left. Neighbours had ready ears and contact with security police. Six years later Lydia was to begin working with SU in Prague as our first staff worker in Eastern Europe.

Living and working in Wrocław in southern Poland, Ruth Kowalchuk had been persuaded in the early days of the eighties to come to the children's and young people's camps to help with translation and interpretation for the various British visitors. Ruth's brother Krysztof, a Baptist pastor, faithfully translated children's SU notes from German to Polish in the late eighties, and these were soon to be published by the Baptist Union in Poland. By 1990, notes for the first two years had been published and a third year was ready for printing. Teenage notes followed as Krysztof worked with a team from Krakow and Wrocław. All this was done in the face of rising costs and the need to find funding. These children's and youth resources were to become invaluable in SU's growing work through a network of denominational and interdenominational camps throughout Poland in the early nineties.

Ruth's enthusiastic participation in the children's and youth camps at Bielice led her inevitably to embrace and take to her heart ministry among young people. And so began the seed of an idea which was to blossom into a spiritually fruitful project: the launching of the Wrocław School of Languages, a school dedicated to relational evangelism where many teenagers and adults came to study English, and where many would find God. Ruth was its founder and first director. Jim Hartley of SU England, an experienced and sensitive trainer, accompanied me on a trip to Poland in 1990 and met Ruth, and there began a friendship which bore fruit in Jim's commitment to training Christian leaders in new and innovative ways of communicating the good news of Jesus, through small groups in language school and camps.

*

It was to be another four years before I travelled again to Poland in 1988. I wrote in my personal log that 'we left the white cliffs of Dover early in the morning of June 28th'; we continued in a car filled with all sorts of Christian resources (mainly theological books), foodstuffs, medicines etc. through Germany to Poland and from there to Czechoslovakia and on to Hungary, returning via Austria, southern Germany and France – and arrived back in the UK twelve days later with one extra passenger! In all we travelled 3,380 miles. I guess this was my longest ever car trip.

I was accompanied by Tim, my younger son, who was a fluent German speaker, and Denise Trotter, who had recently left the SU staff following four years of pioneering work in primary schools in the north of England. We spent the first night in Marburg, where we met Doris Oehlenschläger and discussed some final arrangements for the IFES/SU European high schools conference later in the summer, to be based in Maulbronn in southern Germany. Twelve days later we were to break our return journey at Schloss Mittersill, a key Christian centre in the Austrian Tyrol, where a wide range of student and graduate conferences were held over the years, and where we shared the names of Hungarian students due to attend the IFES Mittersill conferences later in the summer.

From a cosy night in Marburg, we travelled on to southern Poland, to Wrocław and Katowice where we held preparation meetings for the Polish high school students planning to attend the Maulbronn Conference. The process in obtaining the required documents and the transfer of funds for young people from Eastern European countries was anything but straightforward, and invitations to those hoping to participate in conferences had to be sent some months before the event. Disappointingly on this occasion and out of an original list of twelve from Poland, it looked as if there would only be three or four able to make it to the conference, and probably no one would be able to come from Czechoslovakia, where the weakness of the banking system and the transferring of funds was a major issue. Naturally we did not foresee then that in November in the following year, the situation would change dramatically with the fall of the Berlin Wall. Yet I was determined to find and train potential leaders among the Christian young people of these countries and, through prayer, discussion and agreement with IFES staff throughout Western and Eastern Europe, to encourage the appointment to the new student movements of staff who could work with high school students.

Denise's expertise in children's work was invaluable; she had opportunities in all three countries (Poland, Czechoslovakia and Hungary) to share practical ideas with groups of Sunday school teachers and more informally in meeting a number of individual teachers.

From Wrocław, where we first stopped to make some personal contacts with the Zachanovic family, we then made a lightning visit to Katowice, further east and south. There we met Mirek Pieska, the leader of the IFES/ChSA Christian student movement in Poland, with whom we had hoped to stay overnight. Even before we reached Mirek's home, we queued almost two hours to fill up with petrol. Our plans to stay in Katowice overnight didn't seem to fit in with Mirek's plans! However he kindly sent us off to Ustroń, a town very near the Czech border, and gave us the name and address of someone who might help and who also could be interested in meeting us and hearing about Scripture Union.

The family in Ustroń immediately welcomed us and invited us to share an evening meal with them; they naturally asked us where we were staying the night. We had to admit that we didn't know; they insisted that we stay with them without as much as a moment's hesitation. During the evening Ryszard (husband and father), with whom we discussed at some length the nature and practice of children's ministry in Poland, took us into the garden where he was preparing to mow the lawn. I looked at the lawnmower, the like of which I had never seen before, and asked him which make it was. 'I made it myself,' he replied. 'You see, we Poles are individual entre-preneurs by nature!' That phrase stuck with me over the next few years, as I struggled to shape a robust SU movement in Poland and to bring together Christians from different groups and denomina-tions, many of them very effective yet individual 'Christian entrepreneurs'.

Travelling from Poland, we spent the next day on one of my briefest visits to Prague. Quite late on in the evening we drove on to Brno, where we had hoped to meet a pastor. However it was midnight before we found our hotel and we had to leave promptly at 6am to get to the border before our twenty-four-hour transit visa ran out. So a short night in Brno and a tedious wait at the borders while the Czech processed our papers. On to Budapest, where we negotiated the bridges and drove through only one red traffic light, before finding the Bernhardt family.

Dora, one of the daughters, was beginning to work with MEKDSZ (the IFES movement in Hungary) and we had some good conversation about working with high school students in Hungary. Her parents were delightful, gracious Christians, who had faced more than a generation of hostility and opposition to their Christian witness and who now welcomed us into their home. The IFES movement in Hungary had just held their first high schools camp – twenty-four students and a number of leaders; John Samuel from England had been the main speaker. With at least one person coming to faith in Christ, overall this had been a real encouragement to the leaders and in particular to Anna Bernhardt (Dora's sister), who was beginning to pioneer high schools work in Hungary. Ten high school young people would come to Maulbronn – they experienced only minor difficulties over permission to travel.

Forty-eight hours later we set off for Austria, where we broke the night in the comfort of Schloss Mittersill and in the middle of a Christian student conference. The following morning we continued our journey to Bregenz near the German/Swiss/Austrian border, where we stopped for a picnic on the shores of the Bodensee, and then on to SU France's camping centre at Le Rimlishof in Alsace. We ate and slept well at the SU campsite before driving through to the channel port. We had an additional passenger – Evi, the oldest daughter of Bulcsú and Eva Széll – who was coming to England for some weeks, to improve her English and to attend some SU summer events.

1989 took on a different shape. Who would have anticipated the seismic political changes of the late eighties and early nineties? Yet there were many telling indicators when I travelled to Poland in the autumn of 1989.

Some weeks before, in the summer of that year, Valerie and I had stood on both sides of the Berlin Wall on a memorable day, the 11th August. Twenty-eight years earlier to the day had witnessed the closing of the East/West German borders and the dividing of Berlin.

Konstanty Wiazowski. Krysztof Bednarcyk and Aniko Williams at the celebration of the launch of the Wrocław Christian School of Languages, 1989

Jan Tolwinski and his two daughters with the children's Bible reading notes Udany Start

The Wall stood as a vivid and terrible symbol of a divided city and continent. We were accompanied by Bryan and Jean Hogg, good friends from our church in Watford, as we visited Berlin for a few days. Nonchalantly, Valerie spoke to the West German border guard at Checkpoint Charlie, as he stood not more than six feet from his East German counterpart and on the other side of a line in the road. 'Nein,' he almost whispered, when Valerie casually asked him, in the best German she could muster, whether he ever conversed with his opposite number. Later that day we took – unknowingly – an 'illegal' short journey on a train to the outskirts of East Berlin ...

The differences between the two halves of Berlin were stark, not simply in superficial outward appearance. East Germany was called, in the German media (after the Wall fell), 'the most perfected surveillance state of all time'. Some estimates had a ratio of 1 informer for every 6.5 citizens. The Stasi (East German security police) was 'the mainstay of State power. Without it and without the threat of Soviet tanks to back it up, the East German regime could not have survived'.[3]

A few weeks later, in the autumn, I was back in Berlin en route to Poland – a memorable trip when Central Europe was about to witness, in the space of three or four months, fundamental and far-reaching changes to the political scene which had endured in most of these countries for over forty years.

I took the scheduled flight to Berlin. At this time, Tegel was a relatively small and underused airport, but symbolic of a tiny 'island' of western democracy in a sea of Marxist rule. On the bus to the centre of West Berlin (the East German state always emphasised the difference; *Berlin* was the capital of the German Democratic Republic), I was reflecting on the purpose of this visit. I would join with others in Wrocław at the ceremony for the opening of the Christian language school, and participate at the IFES student conference in Warsaw.

I had underplanned the details of my journey, expecting to pick

---

[3] Anna Funder. *Stasiland*. London: Granta, 2003

up a train from Berlin to Wrocław without too much trouble. At the West Berlin Zoo station, dirty and functional in those days, I staggered, under the weight of the familiar heavy bag, from the platforms to the more popular luggage lockers, waiting to pounce on the first empty one. I had been informed at the ticket office that the next train, due to leave at 2.30 in the afternoon for Wrocław, was fully booked. It looked as if I would have to wait for an evening train – getting to my destination in the middle of the night. Nevertheless, in hope, I purchased a ticket and, for an enforced hour of thinking, praying, waiting and drinking coffee, I stayed in McDonald's where thankfully there were seats!

Two o'clock came and the crowds were gathering on the platform on which the overbooked Poland-bound train would arrive. When the train came in, it was deceptively empty and I wondered, *Is this a miracle?*

My joy was short-lived as I was unceremoniously dumped out of this train at East Berlin's Hauptbahnhof. Struggling with my bags through crowds of people on the platforms and underpasses, and with strong rumours of another Poland-destined train, I strengthened my resolve and found my way to the waiting train. No seats were available, but in the face of the attempts of the East German police to stop anyone getting on the platform where the train was waiting to depart, I had used my British passport as a vital piece of equipment in a (unusual for me) charm offensive!

I reached a coach where a few of the passengers helped me find a precious space in the corridor. It wasn't the greatest rail journey I had ever made, standing in a smoke-filled corridor for four to five hours. But in spite of language problems, my companions, who were almost entirely Polish, were friendly and thoughtful. Two young people not only advised me not to attempt to travel on to Wrocław that night, but carried my heavy bag between them a kilometre or so to the nearest hotel in Poznań, where I had to leave the train in any case as it was bound for Warsaw. Poznań was unknown to me, busy and dark. I would have struggled without their help. God's angels?

From the relative luxury of the hotel, I attempted to phone my hosts in Wrocław, but they were not at home. I tried another old friend from the 1980s camps. Her father answered but he spoke only German. Fortunately they had an English student in their home and he conveyed the message to Adam and Mira, the pastor and his wife at the Baptist church, who were able to save Alex Williams a long and fruitless wait on a cold windy station platform late at night.

At lunchtime the following day, Saturday, I arrived in Wrocław to be met by Alex, clad in a pair of lederhosen which he had purchased in Poland for the equivalent of £3. We soon arrived at a building site of the Second Baptist church, where the Wrocław Christian language school would be formally opened and dedicated that day.

Two of those present on that occasion were Krysztof Bednarcyk and Konstanty Wiazowski. Krysztof, the brother of Ruth Kowalchuk and the translator of SU notes, was in good form but suffered from a severe heart condition, and appeared physically worn out by the long-term pressure of working against the stream in a strongly nationalistic, Catholic culture and against the background of all the repressiveness of a Marxist regime. Sadly he died three years later at the age of sixty-four. His passing was a significant loss to the evangelical cause in Poland, where he had always sought to bring people together and to maintain a truly interdenominational vision.

The remainder of my time in Poland during that autumn trip was spent in Warsaw, where the first Polish student conference was being held. Mirek Pieska and his colleague, working with ChSA, the 'new' Polish Christian student movement, had been involved in a minor accident on their journey from Katowice to Warsaw; they hit a stray dog, damaging their vehicle and putting extra pressure on both of them in the run-up to the conference.

During the conference I met with a number of people interested in supporting the IFES ministry in high schools as well as a few high school students, for whom we ran a couple of seminars. The evenings saw a diet of Bible teaching, testimonies, announcements and loud bands! By this point in the eighties the number of Polish

Christian bands and singers was proliferating, making CDs, planning gigs, travelling the length and breadth of the country. A worn-out Marxist culture had no answer to these brave and enduring Christian initiatives.

At the end of my visit to Poland, I travelled overnight by train to Berlin. Two Polish businessmen in the adjacent compartment were friendly and talkative. When, without explanation, we came to a sudden halt about four miles from Friedrichstrasse (the final destination in East Berlin), we had an amusing half an hour or so trying to beat the system by setting out to walk along the rail lines to a local suburban station. We were stopped in our tracks and told in no uncertain terms to get back on the train. This all cemented our friendship.

Eventually arriving at our destination, I looked out of the mud-spattered train window to catch sight of the queue of many hundreds waiting to get through the customs barrier. What hope to catch the flight from West Berlin in a few hours? At that point my new Polish companions took charge! They escorted me with them as they had business visas and the business passport/visa check queue was short and swift. As they persuaded the officials to let me through, they described most of the others waiting for hours to get into West Berlin as part of Poland's 'economic Dunkirk'!

*

Konstanty was a wise senior Baptist leader and had a remarkable capacity to nurture good links across the denominations. From time to time he visited Watford, my home town, to spend some days with Tony Koscieka, a retired pastor who had been involved in itinerant preaching amongst the Polish communities in England and in preparing Polish-language programmes for Christian broadcasting in Europe (Koscieka's letter to a Polish pastor was the piece of 'evidence' that caused us some trouble at the border in 1981, as I wrote in my introduction). Konstanty lived with his wife and family in a small flat near the centre of Warsaw, part of the complex owned by the Baptist Union of Poland and the church to which John Laird referred in the report of his visit in the sixties. Latterly Konstanty spent some time lecturing at the Warsaw Baptist theological seminary, on the outskirts of Warsaw.

During my subsequent visits to Poland over the next six years, he and his wife offered me warm and selfless hospitality; at the same time, he expressed concerns that we were accumulating a large number of unsold children's and young people's Bible reading notes. Wojciech Muranty, our first Polish SU staff worker, tried hard to sell these at the various church conferences. His links were mainly with the Free Evangelical Churches, a small Protestant denomination with fewer than forty congregations throughout Poland at that time. An additional complication was that the notes were seen as a Baptist 'product' as the Baptists had originally been commissioned to publish these. With hindsight I felt that this was a misjudgement. For many years during the communist era, most of the Protestant churches were required to belong to what was called the United Evangelicals. The Baptists and the Lutherans, curiously, were permitted to remain outside this grouping and as a consequence there seemed to be a degree of 'loving suspicion' between these groups. This meant that it wasn't going to be easy to set up an SU committee truly cross-denominational in character. However, leaders such as Konstanty Wiazowski, Krysztof Bednarcyk, Adam and Henryk Krol were exemplary in their commitment to SU ministry and thoroughly ecumenical in their outlook.

Piotr Zaremba, a Baptist pastor, lived in the western Polish city of Poznań with his wife and two small children. He was given to rising early to work on the translation of Christian books for subsequent publication, a vital ministry providing resources for pastors and Christian leaders. His primary calling, however, was local church ministry. Many Christian pastors had to supplement their modest salaries by engaging in other forms of employment.

I invited Piotr to weigh up the possibility of his becoming our SU adult notes translator. The children's and young people's notes had been translated from German. I felt that we should use English-language material for the adult material, while always being open to working with others who would become our first Polish writers.

Zaremba was attracted by the English *Alive to God* adult notes and the first year's notes bore fruit for his labours.

Over the early years (post-1989) of 'freedom' in Eastern Europe, I travelled many times to Poland to encourage Wojciech in what in reality was a lonely task. We would journey by (fast!) car to various towns and cities wherever there was a possibility of making fresh links with church leaders, with a few people involved in Christian publishing and naturally with the ChSA Polish student movement, with whom, for some years at least, we co-operated closely in attempting to develop an effective high schools ministry. Pavel Gumpert and Lea Kjeldson (IFES), working in the south, and Iza Has (SU), working in the north-east, sought bravely to establish links with Christian young people in school. Iza and Lea had planned some training seminars, a high school leaders' winter camp in Wisła, and 'outreach' activities in schools with music and lectures. Links with other Europeans working in predominantly Catholic countries were going to be important for modelling good practice. Pascal Hickel in France and Fernando Caballero in Spain had a combination of accumulated wisdom and good models to share.

My volunteer colleague, a young vibrant Australian, Alison Houghton, came with me on at least one visit to Poland. *Now I'm a Christian*, an attractively designed and illustrated book written by Jim Smith, had been a successful teenage/student resource published by SU in England. We both recognised its potential for helping Christian young people in addressing some very practical and down-to-earth questions about living a fruitful and faithful Christian life while at school or university. It took patience and several false starts before we saw the publishing of this book in Polish – all 5,000 copies. Translation had been a challenge; some aspects of Jim Smith's writing were fairly deeply enculturated in a western setting, and different Polish translators seemed to find difficulty in establishing an effective and usable translation. But in the end Mirek Pieszka, the dynamic leader of the student IFES/ChSA movement in Poland, helped solve our problems and we published the book early in 1995. How many copies we sold, gave away, or stored in the warehouse and for how many years, I simply cannot say! It is enough to note that the publication of a good and useful book was by no means the end of the story; the distribution and promotion of Christian literature was always going to be problematic. The initial sales were a little disappointing.

Meanwhile in Poznań, Piotr Zaremba had been working on the translation of *Alive to God*. By late 1993, when we met with him at his compact flat, he was ready to write at least some of the *Alive to God* notes and invite others to assist rather than continuing to translate and adapt from English. But one year later, it appeared that progress had been disappointingly slow; two writers were committed, but would they get the first quarter of the notes published by 1st January 1995? And this was not the only challenge. Promoting the concept of regular personal Bible reading and 'cracking' the problem of the distribution of these resources to the churches and groups was never going to be easy. Protestant church life could be fractured by all sorts of external and theological influences; uncertainty, lack of knowledge and more than occasional mild suspicion between denominations didn't always help in promoting and fostering the aims of Scripture Union Poland.

Before he died in 1992, Krysztof Bednarcyk had faithfully continued to translate the third year of both *Guterstart* (German-language children's Bible reading notes – *Udany Start* in Polish) and *Geradeaus* (German-language teenage notes). Finance was always a problem in printing, marketing and selling. The notes were cheap by western standards (around one third of a DM), but five copies cost the equivalent of the monthly average salary in Poland. I wrote in my log at the time (1990), 'We have submitted an application for a grant to "Feed the Minds", though I believe at best we are unlikely to get more than 3000DM.' This kind of grant could make all the difference when coming to sell these resources at a price that people under significant financial pressure might afford. In general, translators and designers were not paid for this work on the children's and young people's Bible reading notes; they saw this as a volunteer ministry and they passionately believed in the value of leading children and young people to engage with the Bible!

Around the same time, *Introduction to the Bible* by Ernst Aebi was translated into Polish. Aebi, an SU pioneer leading the Swiss SU movement for many years, had agreed this in collaboration with Joseph Riffert, one of the first intrepid travellers to Eastern Europe in the seventies and eighties. Andrej Komraus, a quiet but godly leader in the Polish Methodist Church, was responsible for getting this book published.

Jim Hartley, from Bury St Edmunds, of whom I have written earlier, was a valued member of the SU England training department and over the ensuing years he made an enduring and fruitful link with the Wrocław School of Languages. Jim was a key player in the development of the evangelistic language 'camps' run for the students at the school. He spent many hours training and teaching the Polish volunteers in ways of building bridges into the lives of the students through a relational approach. In November 1990, Ruth wrote, 'As far as the camps are concerned we have made Jim Hartley responsible for the staffing of the camps and I direct everyone to him as the co-ordinator.' Thus for several years Jim played a vital role and by 1994 I had written in my log, 'Through Jim's involvement in the language camps of the Wrocław School of Languages he has been instrumental in bringing into being a strong group of young adult Christians eager to serve with SU.'

In October of that year (1994) Jim, who had travelled with me in Poland for some of my time there, spoke at the English-language service at Wrocław Baptist church, where the language school was based. Following an interview with the press, SU had had some good publicity in one of the three city daily newspapers. The service was attended by over a hundred (mainly) young people, and several requested Bible reading notes. Afterwards a small group of young adults met with us and we shared the potential for their involvement in promoting regular Bible reading amongst young Christians at the language school who they were discipling, as well as working through their own links in the city. There seemed to be great potential in all this. Yet what would be the longer-term results? This was a recurring question in my mind, even after the most encouraging encounters with others who showed promise. Who would follow this up effectively?

During the early and mid-nineties, I sought to build good and positive relations with the ChSA student movement leaders based in Katowice. We made plans and outlined strategies. Lea, Pavel and Iza worked hard and faithfully in the high schools ministry. Yet they all lived at a distance from one another and communication was never going to be easy. Additionally there were daily pressures on people with full diaries and less than the required human and technological resources available to accomplish their visions. There was too much to do, too many people to meet and talk to in the space of a twenty-four-hour day, too few people to assist in the work to which God had called them, and ever-limited financial resources. Yet for all that, God was working powerfully in the lives of university and high school students.

By the mid-nineties, we recognised that the SU movement in Poland was struggling. Members of the committee were engaged in many activities apart from Scripture Union. Sometimes our two staff members felt lonely and unsupported, and understandably were limited in their vision and capacity to create new ways of working.

Following a number of visits to Poland in the first part of that decade, in 1995 I travelled to Dzięgielów at the invitation of Henryk Krol, one of the SU Poland committee whose DEO recordings studio was producing Christian CDs and videos as well as launching radio broadcasts, sensitively produced and directed by a gifted team. Dzięgielów was a small town in southern Poland where for a few years a growing Christian convention had been held in the summers. Around 5,000 people gathered each day for Bible teaching and evangelistic outreach – a great mix of denominations including Catholics and Protestants. SU Bible reading notes were promoted at the main sessions, and at one of these I was invited to speak briefly (around seven minutes!) about SU. There was a good and encouraging response; a few wrote down their names and addresses, expressing interest in being involved; several asked for further information about SU in Poland. But my question was 'How well will this be followed up?' In a few days I would be flying back to the UK. The Polish SU staff were only able to be present at the convention for a relatively short time; I sensed this might be yet another missed opportunity.

Henryk had arranged for me to conduct seminars in Bible engagement, and each day we worked with forty to sixty people eager to engage with scripture and to discover new ways of encountering reading and applying God's word. Malgosha, a young Catholic medical practitioner, was so eager for her husband and her daughters to come into a living faith and start reading the Bible. Lesznek, a married man also from the Catholic Church, had given his life to Christ during the convention; he offered to help translate into Polish a short English-language SU Bible reading booklet *Ready to Serve*. Lesznek was a thoughtful person, asking good, important questions. Yet in this context, what was the best way to follow up these young enthusiastic believers? Henryk Krol and his wife Bogusha and three children were fully committed, Henryk working at a phenomenal pace – sixteen-hour days for six or seven days each week without real breaks. Never was I more convinced that we desperately needed a fellowship of committed volunteers in SU Poland, not just to build a strong SU movement, but to be on the front line, building relationships with individuals and families in need, harnessing the energies and enthusiasm of those who were prepared to get involved.

While staying at Dzięgielów for several days, we held an SU committee, sharing some of our concerns about the slow growth in SU Poland. Much had been attempted; most of us had high expectations and there had been some disappointments. It was agreed that we should look for a new leading staff member who might take the movement on into the next stage. Tomek Blazowski, who had attended the student camp at Bielice in 1984, where Alex and I had been involved, was now a pastor of a Baptist church, not so far from

Dzięgielów. Henryk spoke highly of him and a year later Tomek joined the SU staff. Tomek was entrepreneurial and was enthusiastic, committed to winning young people for Christ. In the winter he worked on the ski slopes of the Tatras as a ski instructor, seeking to reach out to the younger generation. Yet he found administration irksome and his wife assisted with this over the years.

After some years, Tomek moved on and Chris became the leading staff worker. The Indian village project for children was developed and eventually a sports ministry was pioneered. A young woman, Kaja, whom I met at the international SU teen games event in 2012, held in East London in the shadow of the Olympic Games, was committed to developing this ministry for SU Poland. Later Kaja was able to travel to the Living Hope SU conference in Malaysia and from there began to work with young people. Kaja continues to recruit and train young leaders (aged sixteen to twenty) who are involved in summer and winter camps and events during the school year for children and young people.

While Scripture Union no longer had an official status in Poland, it had an informal but active 'presence' through Kaja and the volunteer team. In a European bulletin (January 2016) they asked for prayer for 'The Group of our young leaders (called Delta) for the age group of 12–16 year olds: that they will grow in their relationship with Jesus more and more, and that their motivation to serve people will be based on love that is dwelling in their hearts', and for 'The winter camp taking place in January/February. For a good preparation process and great leaders serving there, so that God's love will be shared abundantly.'

Balkan Ventures:
Healing and Spinach

———— ᥱᦔ ————

I landed in the crowded, cramped and smoky atmosphere of the air terminal at Sofia on a warm afternoon, in late April 1991. David Jones, SU's general director in the USA, had been in touch with me some months before, asking if I could meet up with Bonnie Campbell, a young woman pioneering community Bible study, with whom David Jones and SU USA had had some close links and useful discussions about ways they might work together. A few weeks earlier, I had met Bonnie in Poland, where I had introduced her to some church contacts. However, by this time, I was uncertain as to how effectively our two organisations might work together. My support group back home had been quietly enthusiastic about this idea; it always seemed to amaze them that there were so many mission agencies 'operating' in Eastern Europe, each seemingly treading their own independent pathway.

Bonnie was a gifted young woman with a pioneering heart. Community Bible study – an integrated church-based programme of personal and group study – had been the vision of her mother. Before arriving at Sofia airport, where we had agreed to meet, Bonnie had travelled on her own to Romania where through Elizabeth Ton, the wife of Baptist pastor and leader Joseph Ton, she had had a fruitful few days and established some roots for her ministry in Oradea. I guess that her visit to Poland had been less encouraging. In Warsaw, while I sat and silently prayed for her, the council of the Church of Evangelical Christians had listened politely to her presentation, but had remained cautious about what seemed to them yet another American mission agency attempting to create a foothold in that part of the former communist empire.

Bonnie, who had been due to land in Sofia a little before my flight, was nowhere to be seen. Nic Nedelchev, a bright and bustling Baptist pastor, had arranged to meet me – but, as ever, I had feelings of apprehension coupled with a certain amount of anticipation and excitement walking into entirely new territory.

Just as I was beginning to feel helpless, Nic – who I had not met before – appeared. It was always astonishing how we managed over the years to identify ourselves in different countries. Before the changes in November 1989, we were generally extremely cautious – a thoughtless mistake could have proved not just embarrassing but a little costly to our hosts. After the changes, occasionally I had rather self-consciously held up the SU logo and sometimes the name of the person who was meeting me. But God always managed to organise it so that our eyes made contact and instant recognition was usually accompanied by laughter and handshakes.

Nic asked where Bonnie was. We waited a further five long minutes before she suddenly appeared. She couldn't put up with the smoke and the crowds, so had been standing outside in the relatively fresh air.

Nic took us to our respective apartments and left us. Years before the advent of mobile phones, I had no obvious means of connecting either with Bonnie or Nic, so I just waited patiently in the quite pleasant but dark room, one of numerous 'rooms' available now to foreigners for a modest price. We were due to speak at a meeting early that evening; clearly Nic was a very busy man and everything would be cut fine, timing-wise. Would we eat before the meeting?

Whereas some of the other countries had had links with SU over the past fifty or more years, we could find no such links in Bulgaria. Joseph Riffert, who had worked covertly but effectively on behalf of SU Europe in the mid-eighties, had not been able to travel to Bulgaria. Much earlier, SU reading cards had been published in the Bulgarian language, in London. How these were distributed, no one seemed to know – perhaps via known pastors and church leaders, or through short visits made by missionaries from the UK? In recent months before this initial visit, some Bulgarian Christians had written to me and I had planned to meet them. Helen Parry, whom I had not met before, but who was known to some of my SU colleagues in Yorkshire, was an English teacher who had gone to Bulgaria and was teaching English in a secondary school in Sliven some 200 miles east of the capital. But first there were some opportunities and unexpected encounters in the capital city, Sofia.

Where Nic Nedelchev had deposited us was a bleak area of Sofia – outside the more interesting central area, with its historic buildings and defaced Leninist monuments. The skyline in this twilight zone of Sofia's inner suburbs was a veritable forest of Eastern European ten-storey dwellings, faceless solutions to a long-term housing problem: identical 'blocks' for hundreds of families, often surrounded by a mini-wasteland patrolled by dogs and by small boys in search of any discarded bottles, or indeed any other waste materials that might prove financially lucrative! Enterprising families, such as the one I stayed with, registered with the tourist office and made some highly prized dollars from letting their one 'spare' room.

Nic eventually arrived, with Bonnie, to take us not to the restaurant but straight to the Baptist church, where we would launch into an as yet unplanned programme with unknown people, mainly young adults. The idea had been that we would lead a series of seminars over the weekend on children's and youth work. It seemed less than well organised when we arrived, with no one ostensibly in charge. Nic quickly departed for other church business, and left us to it – whatever 'it' was to be. We were hungry, but there was no food in sight – just a few biscuits and drinks.

At this point I imagine Bonnie and I independently realised that any plans and prepared programmes we had made meant little. The only solution was to ask the group there and then what they wanted us to do. The result was an 'unstructured' session on evangelism. But (to me at least) it felt like a muddle; where were they coming from and what had we to offer? Was it really relevant to a newly religiously liberated but incredibly poorly resourced Christian community? At the end of the evening I wasn't sure what we had accomplished and felt more than a little discouraged. The following day was meant to be a continuation of the programme, but it transpired that many who were there on Friday evening were not free to come back in the morning (was that their excuse for missing another poor meeting?); others would come who hadn't been in on the Friday evening's sessions.

Nic eventually came back for us on that first evening, tumbling to the fact that neither of us (nor he, for that matter) had eaten anything that day. We ended up in a Bulgarian version of a transport café, eating bits of pizza off rough – but clean – pieces of cardboard! It was welcome!

The following morning was more promising; twenty people came, some from the previous evening, others who had not been free on Friday evening. I began with a thirty-minute session describing and illustrating the 'SU method' in systematic Bible reading; later in the morning, I led a session for Sunday school teachers. Bonnie began with a session on 'friendship evangelism' and followed that with practical teaching on group Bible study. We finished at lunchtime. Yanita, the leader of the Baptist church Sunday school, had asked me to speak to the children the following morning (Sunday). After a lunch with Ilia, explaining what Scripture Union was and did, we retreated to the plush Sheraton Hotel to make phone calls, drink coffee and change money. Then to my apartment to prepare for Sunday.

The Sunday school was a riot! By rearranging the furniture, mostly heavy and unused church pews, I got the children into the 'boat on the Sea of Galilee' and we managed to make a fair amount of noise battling against the wind and the waves. I applied the story simply. The conditions of the room, with more than sixty children of a variety of ages present, did not exactly lend themselves to interaction. Yet the children had fun and hopefully they learned and were reminded of the all-powerful God who can control and oversee the circumstances of life! Afterwards an American IFES visitor who had been in the church next door said, when I told him we had had a lively time, 'Yes, we could hear you throughout the service!'

The remainder of the time in Sofia was taken up with (mostly informal) meetings, inevitably punctuated with translation, which slowed down the process and gave me time to think about the next thing I wanted to say. But was what I was saying and explaining being understood? I met with denominational leaders, sharing the SU vision and gently probing to see whether it had any 'spiritual resonance' here in Bulgaria. Naturally, I was keeping an eye open for people who might commit themselves to getting involved with SU in Bulgaria, but was all this too premature? Meetings were held in discussion with new Christian publishers who were on the lookout for good-quality materials. Stoyko Petkov of Studio 865 was producing innovative audio and visual material and wanted to adapt some of SU's cassettes and videos. Yet when I left Sofia, I felt that establishing SU here would be a real struggle. There were so many mission agencies with a wealth of resources and seemingly unlimited funds that we in SU simply could not expect to match. On the other hand, were there other qualities that some might value, and opportunities that we should, with integrity, exploit for the kingdom?

A sunny, gentle stroll in central Sofia with Helen Parry and Kiril Christov

Generally, I had been rather too optimistic about getting around on my own by public transport in Eastern Europe. Nic was too busy to organise my travel, but he did drop me off at the main rail station in Sofia on my departure for Sliven, 200 miles east of the capital, yet with no precise instructions as to how I should purchase a ticket. In the end buying a single ticket to Sliven was surprisingly but deceptively easy. Cyrillic lettering made finding the platform and the right train tricky; once on the right train, finding a seat was a little more challenging. The train seemed crowded. As I stepped up into the coach, I contemplated yet another smoky corridor for a four-hour journey into the heart of this unfamiliar country. No one had suggested that I should have reserved a seat.

Amazingly, in the compartment adjacent to where I took up my pitch in the corridor of this overcrowded train, there was an empty seat. Soon after I sat down on my heavy bag, a man came out of the compartment, and invited me to sit in the empty seat! He apparently had booked two seats, but at the last minute his wife was unable to travel with him. The rest of the passengers, both those sitting down and others standing in the corridor, were not amused – feeling that because I was a westerner, he had given up his seat in order to gain some favour (and perhaps money?). Of course I couldn't understand what they were saying, but body language and looks were sufficient.

Helen Parry met me at Sliven station and took me to the Sliven hotel where she had booked me a room. Superficially it looked fine. At night it was less inviting. Loud music was reverberating against the windows and making it almost impossible to sleep. Restlessly, I turned over in bed, thinking, *There must be a better hotel in Sliven than the Hotel Sliven!*

Helen's tiny flat was an oasis during the day. When she was not teaching, we talked over the different options for developing SU in Bulgaria. She wanted me to meet Tihomir, young leader of the local Pentecostal church, where God had been working in amazing ways.

On the following day, a public holiday, we climbed up a nearby hill to reach what seemed to me to be a vastly superior hotel to the one in which I was supposedly sleeping and breakfasting. There, with Tihomir taking charge, we held a healing meeting. This would be a little outside my comfort zone, I reflected. I had never experienced anything quite like this and was apprehensive.

We stood on the broad top of a high wall adjacent to the large hotel car park, where more than 200 people were gathered. I spoke first – a simple testimony of what God had done in my life based on the tenth chapter of John's gospel. When I stopped speaking and beckoned to an American pastor also visiting Sliven, he did not move but simply whispered, 'You continue, my brother; you have the anointing!' An intriguing observation!

At the end of all the relatively short talks, Tihomir invited those who wanted to experience God's healing touch to raise their hands, then to place their hands on whichever part of their body was in need of healing, and then he prayed – how he prayed! We were to witness some remarkable signs, as God brought many into an experience of Christ the healer and deliverer. But was this what God had brought me to Bulgaria for? What had this got to do with establishing SU ministry? Of course it was early days still and I needed to learn patience. 'Doing' ministry in fellowship with other believers was an important 'incarnational' practice.

This profoundly real experience of witnessing God's power to heal had stirred my heart and mind. A few days later, we experienced, at the mid-week meeting of the Sliven Pentecostal church, the power of ordinary people giving testimony to what God had been doing in their lives in bringing them to wholeness of body and spirit over the past days or even weeks. As I reflected on all that had happened over these days in Sliven, it seemed to me apparent that God was doing a very special work at this 'kairos' time in Bulgaria's history, when illness and disease seemed to have gripped and ensnared the lives of many, and when their human dignity had been compromised by a bankrupt political ideology for more than forty years.

On the day we had climbed the hill to engage in the ministry of healing, I was able to discuss with Tihomir how he might see

Scripture Union being established in Bulgaria as an authentically Bulgarian movement, and whether he thought there was anyone he knew who could do it. He pointed immediately to Helen! Initially, I naturally hesitated as Helen was an 'outsider', a western teacher in her first year of living in Bulgaria. Shouldn't we find a Bulgarian first? Yet perhaps it could work out? Helen was open to the idea and felt positive about SU. She had a good track record in her association and involvement with SU in England; while not yet fluent in Bulgarian, she appeared to be accepted by many in the churches here in Sliven. Could Sliven be a good base for SU, ideally situated in the heart of Bulgaria, with good access to a number of regional centres? I even toyed with the idea of buying a flat for around £4,500 which could be used as an office with accommodation for visitors. Now was the time, as prices were almost certainly to rise within the next two years. On the other hand the purchase of a flat might inhibit later development, especially if we found out that e.g. Sofia would be a more appropriate place to base the movement.

From Sliven, Helen and I travelled to Varna on the Black Sea coast, where we had many moving (as well as a few amusing) moments while witnessing what God was doing in the churches. We met representatives of the Pentecostal and Methodist churches, but not the Baptists, whose leaders had gone to Sofia that weekend. We talked through some of these issues, punctuated by church services, where in preaching I was invited to give an 'altar call' and pray for those who came forward in repentance. At one church an undergarment was thrust into my hands to pray for the physical restoration of an absent 'brother'.

Later, I was accommodated for two nights in what looked like a garden shed, and locked out of the much more substantial house where Helen was sleeping and where we breakfasted. Helen would stay on in Varna for a few days. I took the flight back to Sofia early Monday morning. Having arrived at the sparsely peopled local airport well before the pilot, I spotted him being ferried to the small 'prop' which would take me bumpily back to Sofia. An interesting lunchtime was spent with an aged saintly Bulgarian lady, who fed me with a huge plateful of spinach and a fried egg. 'I hope you like this,' she said, tersely adding, 'but missionaries should eat whatever is set before them'. Twenty-four hours later, back in England, I had an uncomfortable few hours; the consequence of too much spinach or too little sleep?

Danubian Travels

—e9—

In the autumn of 1986, Valerie and I travelled to Budapest. Valerie had always looked forward to joining me on visits to Eastern Europe. We had twenty-five years of marriage to celebrate and I was curious to see and absorb a little of another Central European culture.

On this visit – our first to Hungary – we stayed four nights right in the heart of Budapest, in a typically communist-style hotel on the busy Lenin körút, trams relentlessly rattling past our window every few minutes. Our room was pleasant enough, characterised by the fading grandeur of another era. The hotel was a favourite of Russian visitors and party apparatchiks: mostly men in long black leather coats, looking suspiciously at the other guests. Yet we had no feeling of being unduly observed, and travelled around the city easily, enjoying coffee and gateaux in the cosy little Ruswarm café, a few hundred metres from the finely patterned roof of Matthias Church and adjacent to the Fisherman's Bastion on the hill high above the river Danube, bisecting the city of Budapest and at that time spanned by seven bridges.

We had hoped to make some contact with Bulcsú Széll, a Lutheran pastor living in the country some distance from Budapest. In the event it proved impractical. While these four days were essentially a holiday, we had brought books to give to Bulcsú, with whom I had corresponded for the past few years and who would eventually become the first chairman of SU Hungary.

In the eighties, Bulcsú, his wife Eva and their growing family were pastoring a Lutheran congregation in the rural north of Hungary, in the small village of Lucfalva. As an evangelical, Bulcsú had been dispatched to this remote location by his politically compromised bishop who took the view that his 'gospel' work would cause embarrassment in the influential capital of Budapest, but that it would be ineffective and his witness stifled in this out-of-the-way village. How little the bishop really knew or understood! Over the years, Bulcsú saw a steady number of people of all ages coming to faith in Christ, and a healthy growth in the number of families coming to the church.

Bulcsú was concerned that the children in the village be able to receive basic Bible teaching, and I had been sending him SU teaching materials (*Learning Together*) which he translated into Hungarian. Chris Davies, one of IFES's pioneers in the later seventies and early eighties, had approached me, knowing my interest in Eastern Europe, and we had agreed to send out English copies on a regular basis. Of course it was not possible to publish these in Hungary at that time – Bulcsú simply made rough translations which he laboriously copied by hand for his Sunday school teachers in the small village church, where remarkably, and surely as a testimony to his faithfulness to God, the congregation had grown over the years from twenty-five to almost 250.

On this visit in 1986, as I have said, we had hoped to visit Bulcsú and his family, and deliver the literature which we felt would be encouraging and helpful to him and his church. As we scanned the map we realised that this was an unrealistic journey for us to attempt. So we took the books into a branch of the Budapest post office where they wrapped them up badly. The price of the postage was unbelievably cheap, by British standards. But was there a better and more reliable way to send the books? We never found out, but sadly the books never arrived in Bulcsú's village! A few years later I took more literature; on that occasion I took it by car directly to the village and met Bulcsú in person.

In Budapest, there was another family whom we had looked forward to visiting in 1986. Marta and Agoston Dobos had sent two of their children, Marta and Agoston, to a Scripture Union holiday activity in Colwyn Bay in the early eighties. We had kept in touch over the next few years, and were invited to share a meal at their family home in the fourteenth district. In the midst of the crowded and interesting meal, grandfather Károly arrived and immediately plied me with all sorts of friendly questions. I found out much later that Károly Dobos had visited Scotland in 1947 and had spoken at the church woman's guild in Dollar where I went to school.

Károly stood firm in his faith during the communist period. Before World War II, he had worked with the YMCA in Hungary and had trained as a Reformed church minister. Following the war he continued with the YMCA – a potent force linked to a strong and significant Christian revival in Hungary in the mid-to-late forties when many young people were converted. More recently in retirement he had set up a branch of the Leprosy Mission, based in the Reformed church in Budapest's fourteenth district. Each week the volunteers would meet to prepare parcels of bandages and other medical resources to be sent to Asia. His son Agoston would later serve on the first SU Hungary committee.

In the summer of that year (1986) Bence, another of Agoston and Marta's four sons, would travel to England with his cousin Judit to take part in an SU holiday activity. Both Bence and his brother Agoston trained for the ministry and in the nineties Bence spent some time as an 'apprentice' at Emmanuel Church, Wimbledon. The daughter of Marta and Agoston, Marta, accompanied me on a short visit to Oradea where I first met Nelu Dan, who was to become our SU chairman in Romania. Later Marta led one of the early SU camps for children. All these early connections and friendships were important building blocks in discovering the way to establish a truly national SU movement in Hungary.

Into the Nineties: Innovations and Changes in Hungary

By the summer of 1989, East Germans were flooding into Hungary and then over to the west and to freedom. There was a sense of new beginnings and an exciting anticipation in the air; the atmosphere of a quiet but profound revolution was unmistakable, and the long-endured, tight political restraints were loosening at an increasing pace. The American evangelist Billy Graham had conducted an outdoor crusade in the heart of the capital at the Nep football stadium earlier that year, with encouraging results but poorly organised follow-up.

In the three years since we first visited Budapest in 1986 I had developed some useful links with a number of people in Hungary, and in July 1989 I was invited to speak at a teenage camp being organised by the Mekdsz/IFES schools and student movement in Hungary. In 1988 they had run the first ever high schools camp. The site of the 1989 camp was basic; there was no electricity in what had been a group of farm buildings on the edge of a small town near the Danube, south of Budapest. On dry and hot sunny days, meals and meetings were almost entirely outdoors. Young people were challenged to be Christians who stood out at school; some responded with a depth of commitment that was moving. I wrote in my log at the time:

On the grass bank by the Danube, we sang some Christian songs. I then spoke for 10–15 minutes about Zaccheus (Luke chapter 19); 20 or so young high schoolers listened attentively, along with a dozen or so local boys, mostly on bikes – they had been just hanging around. I couldn't judge what other passers-by made of it all. Sometime after I spoke, and while some of our leaders were engaging with the bikers, one of them asked me how I had become a Christian. Two years earlier, unconcealed witness in such a situation would have been impossible. But now, with the effective dismantling of the communist youth movement, there was a vacuum ready to be filled. Afternoon clubs in schools including Christian ones became a real option. There were increasing opportunities for a re-launching of Christian instruction for school children and young people; but would there be people who would commit time to becoming effective communicators of Christian values and beliefs? If not, would other values and belief systems begin to fill the vacuum? Further, with the learning of the Russian language no longer compulsory in High School, many students are more interested in learning English and other European languages. Hungary is likely to be short of up to 1,000 teachers of English and district education departments may be open to English speaking graduates with TEFL qualifications. How should we respond to all this?

This was the question I was reflecting on as I wrote this part of my log in the airport lounge at Vienna a few days later, waiting to board the slightly delayed BA flight to Heathrow. I concluded in my log, 'Pray that we will move at God's pace – not over-cautious; neither rushing ahead in a wave of enthusiasm without listening carefully to our Hungarian sisters and brothers.'

My travelling to Europe had been pretty intensive over this four-month period. This visit to Hungary had been my sixth visit to Europe since Easter and I had a further planned eight-day visit to Spain for the Spanish GBE high school camp towards the end of July.

The following year provided further opportunities for visits to Hungary to seek to establish a high schools work, which in the early nineties struggled to take shape. Nevertheless, in the summer of 1994, and in temperatures of up to 40°C, a small team of Hungarian high school students and teachers hosted our fourth European high schools conference for more than a hundred students from fifteen countries with thirteen different languages, in the village of Pécel,

Outdoors for meals, meetings, discussions at the high school camp in Hungary,
July 1989

A design for the brochure for the high schools conference in 1994, sketched by a
Hungarian student

on the southern edge of the capital. Overall it was a very important time for many of the high school students and leaders. Chris, an eighteen-year-old, epitomised the response of many as he wrote, 'The greatest thing is not only meeting everyone from other countries, but also to realise that we have the same desire to see our school friends reached with the gospel of Jesus.'

These conferences had been crafted and planned from the early eighties, and their roots went back to the seventies when SU in England launched 'Euroshare', an event involving young people and leaders from three European countries: Norway, West Germany and the UK. Each year, a group of seventy or eighty senior high school students and leaders had met in one of the three countries (yearly in rotation) for friendship, worship and Bible engagement. The German and Norwegian groups were part of the IFES movements working with high school and university students on the continent of Europe. This in turn led to a developing network – initially quite informal but also motivated and inspired by the effective work of Branse Burbridge, who had pioneered SU's work in England and Wales from the mid-forties. By 1976 Branse was appointed as international high schools consultant for IFES. In 1976 in Denmark and again in Germany four years later, Branse organised two groundbreaking conferences for staff members of SU and IFES movements in Europe who were engaged in high schools work. Growing out of all this, an 'informal' group was created, bringing together staff from three or four European movements to create a European high schools 'action/planning group'. Wilfred Ahrens and Doris Oehlenschläger from the SMD (Germany), Sven Holmsen from NKSS, Honor Perfect and Fernando Caballero from GBE (Spain), Daniel Poujol from LLB (France) and much later others from Scotland (David Geddes), Poland (Pavel Gumpert) and Yugoslavia (Melita Vidovic) joined the group. We worked together to shape the future course for Europe-wide events for high school students, staff and volunteers from the European SU and IFES movements as I took over from Branse in 1986, now with a specific brief for Europe.

During the eighties we sought to bring a few 'key' high school students from the 'closed' countries of Eastern Europe; young Christians with a vision of what God wanted to do in their school were invited to join with their brothers and sisters from the west. Getting their visas was always a challenge and up until the day of arrival we couldn't be sure that they would arrive. We used simultaneous translation, mostly pretty effective except on one occasion when someone was giving a talk not easily understood by most of the participants (even those who spoke his language!). The Polish translator sitting in the translation 'booth' had apparently abandoned any attempt to make sense of it. I asked him afterwards how he had coped, since the Polish young people had burst into laughter from time to time during a complicated and serious passage of the speaker's talk. He said, 'Well, it was rather difficult this morning; when I got totally lost, I just ended up telling them jokes!'

Overall, and beyond the seventies and eighties into the mid-nineties, the co-operation between two major Christian organisations (IFES and SU) was significant, reflecting how much

High schoolers from Hungary, Yugoslavia and Poland at the European high schools conference at Maulbronn in Germany, 1991

Hilary Guest (Blair) and Keith Judson with Czech students attending 'Euroshare':
an international event organised annually by SU/SMD/NKSS

more effectively we could advance the cause of the gospel together in diverse situations where our approach to this kind of work was identical and rooted in a shared philosophy of ministry. How might we have sustained this into the twenty-first century?

In Hungary during the early nineties we had discussed, with several church leaders and pastors, how best to serve the churches and the needs of children, young people and families through the ministries of Scripture Union, and how to establish an indigenous Hungarian SU movement. Children's Bible reading notes seemed the priority and by 1993 our first staff worker was appointed – Beata Toth. Beata was an architect by training and had studied theology in Vienna. Living in Budapest, she saw the importance of working with women, and developed 'reading' sessions, when they read and reviewed Christian books with a view to getting some published by Scripture Union.

Bulcsú's brother-in-law, Janos, had developed a strong interest in publishing media resources. We explored ways of making some of the earlier SU videos available in Hungary. Janos was a remarkable person; when I first met him, he was pastor in a small village church some fifty miles north of Budapest. Yet he had started, in quite a basic way, to produce audio and visual materials, and soon established the Zaccheus Media Centre (ZMC) in Budapest's twentieth district. By 1994, ZMC had produced and published no fewer than three SU videos, translating and adapting *Joseph*, *Signposts* and *Mark Time*.

Bulcsú, who was to become SU's first chairman, had moved to Budapest, called to minister to a small Lutheran congregation in the Kispest district, south of the city centre. During my many visits I stayed in the family home in Budapest. His four daughters all travelled to England over the ensuing years and stayed in our home. His son, Bulcsú, was the youngest of the five children and was autistic. The love and infinite patience poured out on 'little Bulcsú' by both parents and sisters was just amazing to witness on each of my visits. Sadly, when Bulcsú reached the age of eighteen, he died from a brain haemorrhage. His father wrote a most moving testimony that I treasure to this day.

During these early years of attempting to set up Scripture Union in Hungary, I tried to spend quality time visiting Christian leaders, listening and always attempting to find out what the best way forward for SU in Hungary would be. It seemed that initially we should begin with the publishing of children's Bible reading notes, from German SU material. We were over-optimistic about sales and probably printed more copies than we could realistically sell or give away. Initially, these were stored in the gallery of Bulcsú's Lutheran church from where they were dispatched to various churches and children's groups. We considered other material, particularly some youth resources books, and eventually some of these were published, with drastically reduced print runs. This of course meant that the 'unit cost' was always high and we had to subsidise to sell.

There was a real need for an office where we could store the books and booklets, and this was eventually located in a small ground-floor flat belonging to Bulcsú. It was there that we met with the first SU committee, as we tried to see how best to respond to the needs of the churches and to stimulate interest in SU – not an easy task when in Hungary SU was almost unknown. There was a certain natural suspicion of western Christian agencies that were not able to offer substantial financial and personal resources; there was also a degree of uncertainty about the concept of 'trans-denominationalism' – working together with different church groups who had had little contact with one another during the communist years. I felt strongly that, until we were able to appoint the first Hungarian SU staff worker, SU in Hungary would remain small and relatively unnoticed.

Back in the summer of 1989, I had met Erzsebet Abrahams, a Christian worshipping in a Reformed congregation in Budapest. Professionally she was principal adviser for foreign language teaching in the Budapest education department. My first reaction – and, as it proved to be, quite erroneous – was to be cautious. I had met more than a few enthusiasts over the years who saw westerners as a gateway to fulfilling their personal dreams and ambitions. But I was soon to find out that this remarkable woman had an indomitable spirit and a determination that brooked no neutral or half-baked answers to her persistent questions and seemingly impossible aspirations! She saw clearly the potential for westerners, with teaching experience and qualifications, to come to Hungary and teach English as a foreign language; within a year or so she had established an effective network of Christian teachers from America and the UK, committed to teaching English in the schools and working with young people. She was a realist; she made the point to me that clergy for the most part were not trained to communicate well with young people, and even those who were trained were frequently too busy to give time to this special opportunity.

Christian denominational schools were being re-established

following the political changes. I worked with Erzsebet to recruit a number of teachers from England. Most stayed for a year but a few stayed longer. David Parker was one such. Erzsebet had set up an English-language Bible study group meeting each Friday at the Reformed church in the fourteenth district. Over the years, David and later Nancy and Stanley Hornsby (who had been actively involved with SU in East Anglia and in retirement spent a year in Hungary) and many others served God faithfully in this pioneer work, which helped to lay some foundations for SU work in schools later in the nineties. Cathy and Stephen Young, who came to Hungary on a business assignment but stayed for a number of years, introduced a monthly fellowship for Christian teachers in their home – this was a good meeting point for many, some of whom had become lonely, the only English person in their provincial town or city. Morag Stenhouse, a former staff worker in SU Scotland, had settled in the south-east of Hungary in the almost unpronounceable town of Hódmezővásárhely, fifteen miles north-east of Szeged. Morag had many opportunities as a Christian in her school and community.

I sensed that Scripture Union in Hungary must not be limited to publishing resources. In 1994, led by Beata Toth and Marta Dobos, we held our first SU camp for thirty ten-to-fourteen-year-olds. Marta had first attended an SU camp in England as a teenager in the seventies. Marta and others were pioneers in the launching of SU camps. This would develop over the next four to six years, when SU in Hungary started the programme of holiday Bible clubs for children.

Most of my visits were centred in Budapest. However there were times when we travelled to Debrecen in the north-east, and beyond to Szeged in the south-east. On one occasion I went to Debrecen to meet Janos, a Reformed pastor who was very excited about an English SU book *Working with Under 5s*, which he had consequently translated and published privately without so much as a word to SU Hungary! I recall that he drove at great speed, such that I could scarcely keep up, following him at up to seventy miles an hour along a rough track in a remote corner of north-east Hungary. When he finally left me, setting me on my way back to Budapest in the rented car, his final words were to look out for the speed trap fifty miles or so down the road!

On other occasions, we travelled to small towns to take meetings in different congregations and to explain and introduce the work of SU. One late afternoon in 1994 when Valerie had accompanied me, we drove back into the northern suburbs of Budapest after spending some hours with Beata, only for Beata to realise that we had to track back north-east to the town of Jászberény, where we were due to speak at a Scripture Union meeting. What did Valerie want to do? She was tired; moreover she had heard what I was going to say at the meetings many times, didn't speak a word of Hungarian and wasn't at all sure that she wanted to visit Jászberény. So she chose what she thought would be the better option of getting herself back to the flat belonging to Stephen and Cathy Young, where we were staying for a few days. Grappling with the unfamiliar metro, she surfaced at Moszkva Tér to hunt down the 61 bus stop and back on a

Valerie and I on the balcony at Cathy and Stephen Young's flat in 1994

bumpy bus ride up the cobbled hill to Cathy and Stephen's – a most comfortable apartment and with a beautiful view overlooking the Buda Hills.

Szeged, a charming and interesting city in south-east Hungary, saw us hold further meetings with one of the Reformed church pastors and some other interested Christians in the city. On Sunday morning I was invited to speak briefly about Scripture Union, after which the pastor would preach in Hungarian. Valerie opted to go out with the children for their group.

Without a strong infrastructure and strong committee, it was not easy to see how SU could really take off. Beata had worked assiduously to create an interest in and commitment to Scripture Union. Her major concern was to publish relevant literature that would meet the needs of a variety of ages. In the autumn of 1995 she very ably hosted the training conference for the staff workers in Eastern and Central Europe, in a stylish centre in the heart of Old Buda. Frustratingly I was waiting for heart surgery and my cardiologist had strongly advised against my travelling at this time.

*

Towards the end of the decade, with the further staff appointment in the person of Erzsebet Komlosi, specifically to pioneer work in high schools, we began to see some new and encouraging signs amongst school pupils.

Erzsebet's grandfather, Sámuel Somogyi, was a good friend of Károly Dobos, of whom I have written earlier. Together with István Pógyor and a few others, they were leading figures of the Hungarian YMCA. They organised programmes and conferences for young people, and many young people committed their lives to Christ through their ministry. But the old communist regime hit hardest those who brought the gospel to young people. They were regarded as 'the most dangerous people', a threat to the totalitarian communist system.

They all suffered for their faith. Károly Dobos was an assistant minister at Fasor Reformed Church in Budapest, but was removed from there, to a tiny village church (Szank) in the middle of nowhere.

István Pógyor was put into prison, and beaten up so severely that he died. Erzsebet's grandfather mysteriously disappeared as he was travelling on a train doing an errand for a family member. He never came home. His body was found a few days later next to the railway line. He had been killed. There is no official record that he was killed because of his Christian work, but it is not a far-fetched conclusion. Erzsebet recounted this incident to me and added:

> The day my grandfather left home and never returned, he had said to his wife, 'This is what I read this morning in my Bible: "Leave your orphans; I will protect their lives. Your widows too can trust in me" (Jeremiah 49:11). So if anything happens to me, or I don't return, I want you to know that this is what God has promised to us. Trust in Him.' My mother was seven years old then and she had an older brother who was twelve, and a little brother who was only one. Did my grandfather know that something was going to happen? Maybe he was threatened, but did not share it with his family, not wanting to cause panic? It is more than interesting that God etched this verse into his heart so deeply that morning before He set off ... And in retrospect, it is very obvious that God has kept His promise: the life of his family was not easy in so many ways, but all three children and all of the eight grandchildren became committed Christians, several of us being in full-time ministry. God is faithful.

Now, in the much freer democratic era, Erzsebet had identified, in meeting and talking to local ministers, a need for something like a children's holiday Bible club. Recruiting teams from the UK and training Hungarian young people, we began a programme of eight to ten clubs each summer from 1997. At the beginning, finding and training volunteers in both the UK and Hungary was no easy task. I spent time in my final two years before 'retirement' twisting the arms of some staff who were already engaged in children's ministry through Spring Harvest and other missions, and persuading them that some of the volunteers who gave their time at Easter events might also like to join the pioneering work in Hungary in the summer. We organised impromptu training sessions in London, Middlesbrough and Scotland, as we prepared the UK teams for action. On her part, Erzsebet worked patiently to build relationships with high school and university students and to convince them that they had an important role to play as Christian volunteers, working with children in the clubs. But English-speaking volunteers came not only from Middlesbrough and Spring Harvest, and from the variety of districts in Budapest and beyond; Antipodeans featured too! An amazing story is told by Erzsebet of her early days with SU; she wrote later:

I must write about the way I met Rachel Shute, our volunteer from New Zealand, because it is a truly amazing story. At the beginning of September, I went to see my friends who had recently moved to Budapest. On the way home I got lost somehow despite the fact that I had been in that area previously quite a few times in my life. There was a big crowd waiting at the bus-stop, so I spotted a friendly looking girl to ask for directions. She said 'Sorry, I can't speak Hungarian.' As she discovered that I could speak English, she offered me her map and it did not take me more than a minute to find the directions I was looking for. Since the bus was still out of sight we started to talk. It turned out soon that she was a scholarship student from NZ at the Music Academy. When I told her that I am a minister, she was really surprised. She explained that she is a Christian and did not know anybody in Hungary, so could I help her to find a church to go to. I invited her to come along to our English language Bible studies at Baross Ter. She was very glad. However that's not the end of the story yet! I asked her if she had ever heard of Scripture Union because I work for SU Hungary. 'Oh yes,' she said, 'I was a volunteer for SU for some years.' And she offered her help to do some work here too. Since then she has been one of our most committed and enthusiastic volunteers, never misses a training session and she has already started an SU group. Isn't that amazing? Later she told me that it was her second day in Hungary when we met. She was standing at the bus-stop feeling absolutely lonely, homesick, in a strange city, with no friends, no Christian support, and on the verge of tears when I bumped into her. And I was at the very beginning of my work with SU – praying for helpers; but it was very hard to find any. Well it's one of those tiny but shiny miracles of God that I still treasure, and it keeps me going even when life seems hard. It was a real encouragement from above.

Prelude to the Velvet Revolution

⸺ℰℐ⸺

In 1985, Valerie and I had planned a visit to Prague – our first joint visit to Central Europe. During that summer, I was involved in running an IFES/SU European high schools training conference in Maulbronn in southern Germany. Valerie, with our daughters Liz and Anastasia, arrived the night before the conference ended, having travelled from Watford to Germany by train and boat. Wearily they climbed down out of the train at 1.30am to find themselves in an almost deserted Heidelberg station. They spotted my lone figure; I had been waiting for an hour or so to meet them and to take them to Maulbronn. The following morning, the final day of the conference, we set out by car to spend a few interesting days in Prague, before driving on to Vienna and subsequently travelling back through Austria to stay with friends in Bregenz.

Our visit to Prague began ominously, with a minor brush with the 'VB' – the Czech police – who promptly and somewhat obnoxiously fined us for going through the Prašná Brána (the Powder Gate) where they were reconstructing the roads around this historic entrance to the Old Town. The police were not in the mood for brokering deals! While we had imagined that they would be happy with British pounds or German marks, they insisted that we pay up immediately in Czech crowns. We had none, but fortunately an Irishman, who had also been stopped and fined, kindly (and possibly illegally) exchanged our western money into the local currency.

While in Prague, we tried to contact the Christians worshipping in a nearby church. We had some Christian literature (in English) and had been told that this church would value the books. So we went to the address and rang the bell. Eventually a young girl came

– she clearly couldn't speak any English. So in silence I handed the books to her; she smiled and closed the door.

This was not my first (nor my last) visit to Czechoslovakia; two earlier 'transit' visits (en route to Poland in the winters of 1983 and 1984) had taken me, with my colleague and IFES associate Alex Williams, to Pilsen, Prague and Kutná Hora. In 1983 we stopped overnight at Pilsen, where I tasted for the first time the world-famous brew! The Pilsen hotel was a draughty barrack-like building (even described thus by the locals) where we slept restlessly for one short night. Kutná Hora, in mid-Bohemia, was our next stop. When we booked into the local hotel, at least a star up from the Pilsen 'barracks', the receptionist examined my passport carefully, looked up and said, 'Ah, you come from Watford, England. How is Watford football club?'

Pavel and Hannah Cerny and their children lived very near the hotel. Entering their home we were graciously welcomed and shown into a room at one side of the house. We began to unpack books we had brought for Pavel. Pavel came back into the room after a while and, speaking quietly, suggested that we move to the other side of the house; 'We have new neighbours on this side, and we can't be sure that they won't inform on us.'

The following year (1984) was not dissimilar as we stepped out of a flat in the southern suburbs of Prague – home of Marta and Pavel Holeka – to be gently reminded, 'Please do not talk as you leave the building as our neighbours spy on us and may report us to the authorities for entertaining western guests.' This was typical of the atmosphere in Czechoslovakia in the early eighties; we travelled through the country with some caution.

In early 1990, Lydia Trnkova, sister of Marta and our first SU staff worker (almost certainly her grandfather was one of the SU note writers in an earlier generation), told of a very different scene when as a family they had returned from a packed, enthralled, joyful Wenceslas Square amidst the celebrations of the velvet revolution in late 1989. Their youngest child, Lydia, on their way home on the metro, repeatedly chanted the name, 'Havel, Havel,' the hero of Czechoslovakia's astonishing and historic bloodless revolution.

Almost seventy years earlier, in 1921, Mr and Mrs Collyer, the English *CSSM* magazine reported, were hoping to extend the work of the Scripture Union to 'the newly named country of Czecho-Slovakia'. In a style that today we might find quaint and which, in its mildly negative references to the Roman Catholic Church, might be offensive to some, they wrote:

> Prague has a population of 800,000 and is considered a very orderly city. It contains 60 Roman Catholic churches, but now people are continually withdrawing from these and going to Evangelical churches ... we attended part of a service held in one of the churches that had just cut itself loose from Rome. The priest was preaching earnestly to a full house, and lots of people were standing. We caught several references to Jan Huss (one of the key figures in the European Reformation of the 16th Century).

Mr Collyer printed and issued 10,000 SU Bible reading cards (the annual reading plan) in 'Czecho-Slovak', thus reviving what was known before the First World War as the 'Bohemian branch'. Soon after the Second World War, the *CSSM* magazine (May–June 1947) reported that the magazine (for children) had 'reached an unexpected constituency'. A Christian worker in Czechoslovakia had written to say that she had translated articles from the magazine and was using them in her own Sunday schools work. 'The Czech children like them very much, and so another link has been forged in the world-wide fellowship of the *CSSM*.' The report went on to tell that 'one of our continental SU workers recently visited Czecho-slovakia ... hoping that there may be further developments and fresh opportunities for the extension of SU activities there'. There is some evidence that *Daily Bread* (English-language Bible reading notes) was translated in a yearly edition around 1950. Nevertheless, with the Iron Curtain descending over Europe, there was no possibility of the fulfilment of that hope for more than a generation.

During the mid-eighties we had attempted to establish covert links with families and friends of SU in Czechoslovakia, including Lydia and her family. Geoff Ovens, a Scripture Union staff member from Bristol who sadly died prematurely in the late eighties, had gone, a little apprehensively, to Czechoslovakia, to hold a 'secret' Sunday school training weekend in the forests sixty miles from Prague. Lydia, her family and friends were there and Geoff faithfully shared SU resources and practical methodologies for helping children learn from the Bible. He kept in touch over the next few years, and encouraged many of those he had met.

Following our family visit to Prague in 1985, my next journey to Central Europe was in 1988 (I have already written about the Polish part of this epic journey) when, with my son Tim, and Denise Trotter, one of our primary schools specialists in SU England, I travelled to Poland and then to Czechoslovakia and Hungary, to meet with people interested in SU. We arrived in the late afternoon in Prague, coming from the Czech–Polish border, where we had been held up by endless bureaucracy and a measure of suspicion.

I had driven in Prague before, but our family visit hadn't taken us much beyond the main thoroughfares. The Prague city map I had brought was somewhat incomplete. I had arranged a meeting with two men from the fledgling IFES student and high schools movement. I had agreed another meeting for Denise at the home of Lydia in the eastern suburbs, so I sent Tim and Denise on by car and equipped with the map! They seemed to run out of streets but found the house eventually, returning triumphant some hours later, with encouraging tales to tell of an impromptu Sunday school training session and a sharing of SU's resources with several from the churches. They had been one and a half hours late, but those who had waited patiently were accustomed to delays and had spent the waiting time drinking coffee and chatting.

In mid-November 1990, following the demise of the Marxist regime in Czechoslovakia in 1989, I landed at Prague airport at just after two o'clock in the afternoon. I was aiming to reach Lydia's family home as soon as possible. Hiring a car was straightforward;

ninety minutes later, and through heavy traffic and a series of wrong turnings, I drove into Voltova, a relatively quiet street in the eastern suburbs of the capital, where the names of most of the streets were physics-related. Lydia and Jan's home had been largely self-constructed: a detached house with a medium-sized garden and Trabant car in the front drive. With its outdated and inefficient two-stroke engine and its poorly constructed bodywork, the 'Trabbie' was classically symbolic of the former East Germany.

However, there was nothing outdated about Lydia's thinking and vision. At this stage she had not yet started working for SU, but was teaching English in a local primary school. Her main interest was to translate SU's English-language teaching materials for Sunday schools and children's groups into Czech. With a bit of careful adaptation, she saw the real potential for this material in the Czech language. This was her passion and calling.

Earlier in that same year, Janet Morgan (SU England) and Claire-Lise de Benoit (SU French-speaking Switzerland) had run a Sunday school teachers' conference in Prague with great success. We sensed that there was scope to repeat this event in other places, but we needed to talk to pastors and church leaders first, to get them 'on board'. What was striking but not surprising was the poverty of interdenominational ministry among the evangelical churches – this meant a tough road ahead even to get a representative SU committee formed.

But my thrust was to see SU in action even before a committee was set up. During the early nineties I made regular visits to Prague, and worked with Lydia to establish an SU base there. Lydia worked from home; her bedroom was her office, where computer and printer sat on a small table. Her husband Jan and her three children Jon, Martina and Lydia were incredibly supportive, and as a family over the years they showed me unstinting hospitality.

On a number of occasions, I would travel from Vienna, usually in a hired car, and spend time with Lydia seeking to resolve some of the practical problems of publishing the teaching manuals. For Lydia, these were going to be vital in raising awareness of good teaching methods combined with a sensitive biblical approach. The aim? To equip Sunday school teachers who had had little training and few opportunities to access ideas and approaches, providing them with the tools to assist a new generation of children in developing a faith that was robust and informed.

Michael Hews has recorded in his history of Scripture Union, *A Tale of Two Visions*, 'Lydia's father had been part of the Czech underground movement combatting the Nazi regime and had spent five years in a concentration camp. His health had never fully recovered; yet he remained cheerful in adversity.'[1] Her mother, Marta, was a faithful believer and after the changes was a willing and committed helper to Lydia in her early work with Scripture Union. Lydia had learnt during the dark days of restrictive totalitarian rule, under a repressive communist regime, to trust in God.

Lydia's parents had met after the end of World War II at the church where her grandfather was the pastor. 'My grandfather brought many people to Christ,' Lydia recounts in a short article in *Catalyst* (the SU international magazine) in 1991. Lydia remembered the hard years of communist rule: 'What I thought, I couldn't say openly, because if we were open we would lose our jobs. They ran two church youth camps but secretly because children's activities were "illegal". There was one Christian girl there, who was a teacher and knew how to work with children; she was a teacher before she became a Christian – otherwise she wouldn't have been allowed to teach.'

All this took place before the late autumn of 1989. Lydia, her textile designer husband Jan and their three young children were amongst the jubilant and defiant crowds in mid-November 1989. They heard Václav Havel, the new hero of liberated Czechoslovakia, speak from a balcony in the centre of Prague and they knew that the long ordeal of the communist years was over. As I wrote almost a decade later in the SU's daily Bible reading notes

---

[1] Michael Hews. *A Tale of Two Visions: The Story of Scripture Union Worldwide.* Scripture Union: 2001

(*Encounter with God*) December 1998: 'They were unable to describe their feelings of elation on the night of November 1989 when the stony faced hard-line Marxist leaders finally capitulated in Prague. For that moment in history was a passing away of an old order that had built a sense of despair and hopelessness over many years ...'

Yet they were also aware of the longer-term decline in Christian belief throughout the country. Before 1939, the largest non-Catholic denomination (the Hussites) had had a nominal membership of around 1 million, but, weakened by a threadbare and irrelevant theology, and compromised by Marxist infiltration, it was now (in the early nineties) around 200,000 in membership and formal in its worship practice. The evangelical church of the Czech Brethren, while not having given great support to the Marxist-leaning Christian peace movement during the forty years of Russian domination, had around 200,000 members. The much smaller but spiritually vibrant denomination, the Free Brethren Church (of which Lydia and her family were members), comprised around thirty-five congregations and a number of 'mission stations'. Other church groups (Baptists, Pentecostals) were also quite small with around 8,000 members. By the late nineties it was estimated that Protestants comprised only around 1.5% of the population (10 million in all), with Catholics (nominally) around 45%. But the Czech Republic had become progressively and deeply secular. The Marxist atheistic pressures may have penetrated deeper into the culture, especially among the older generations, than in almost any other country in Central or Eastern Europe – a major shift from 1921 when the Collyers first visited and introduced SU. Yet interestingly, when my wife and I briefly visited a vast Catholic church in central Prague at 8.30pm on a Sunday in the early September of 2013, the church was packed, mostly with young people receiving communion.

On one of my many visits to Prague in the nineties, I spotted the old 'Trabbie', symbol of socialist egalitarianism, sitting inert in the front garden of Jan and Lydia's home. Following many years of 'two-stroke' service, it had retired gracefully from active service and had been replaced by a Dacia, a more sophisticated Romanian vehicle. In my dreams, I had thought of bringing the Trabant to England and keeping it in my garage as a souvenir of times past. I hate to think what its CO_2 emissions would have been, or whether it would have made the journey and got through customs. No, a great pipe dream – but scarcely realistic. Well into the twenty-first century I sat in the front seat of a non-movable Trabbie in Budapest's Memento Park, in the shadow of Stalin's boots: an outdoor museum of gigantic statues and ghosts of communist dicta-torship that brought back memories of the false hopes and failed aspirations of an empire without transcendence.

After the changes of November 1989, Jim Hartley and I spent our first night in Prague overlooking the historic Wenceslas Square, in the centre of which was the memorial to Jan Palach, who bravely stood for freedom against the background of harsh totalitarian rule back in the late 1960s.

Jim Hartley visiting the Jewish cemetery in Prague

Lydia and Jiri Lukl discussing plans for the future with me

Jim was a valued member of SU England's training and development team and he had travelled with me to Czechoslovakia, to help Sunday school teachers in their work with children. We travelled to Tabor where we met Grazyna and her husband, a pastor in the local Free Brethren Church. Jim was able to share from his experience of training Sunday school teachers. As we left, I asked about the maximum motorway speed limit between Prague and Bratislava. The pastor was quite precise, but forgot to tell me that the maximum speed only related to overtaking in the outside lane. Subsequently, I was caught out by a very polite policeman who carefully explained to me the more complicated rules for the limits of speed on this major highway (which in emergencies had been used as a runway for aircraft!). However, this gentle officer of the law assured me that my fine was a light one as I had only just broken the limit. Later that day, I was fined again, not for speeding but for taking a right-hand turn into a hotel forecourt where we were staying the night in Bratislava. The police were much less friendly and waited sullenly while I was made to go into the hotel and change my currency in order to pay a petty amount. My companion sat silently and securely in the passenger seat and observed with a resigned but faintly amused look on his face.

Bratislava became the capital of Slovakia, created as an independent state on 1st January 1993 after the dissolution of Czechoslovakia. Scripture Union in Central Europe gained a new movement!

During these early years after the changes, others from SU England's national office played their part in helping those in both Slovakia and the Czech Republic. John Grayston and Cathie Smith went out to assist in Bible engagement and children's ministries, training and equipping churches in handling scripture and working with children. Lydia's main task was the translation, publishing and distribution of the Sunday school teaching materials. For this publishing venture, we were grateful to the Women's World Day of Prayer, which raised sufficient funding to make the publishing of this material possible. Overall the projects in other Eastern European countries would require just over £21,000 to complete. Without the generous and substantial gifts from Christian trusts, many of our initial publishing ventures in the Czech Republic and elsewhere would not have been possible. In all these calculations, we did not include the real costs of translation – most of which was done by volunteers of whom Marta, Lydia's mother, and Marta Holeka, Lydia's sister, were two.

Early in the nineties, Lydia had launched an SU camp for young people. The very first camp, of which she spoke memorably at the international SU conference in de Bron, Netherlands, in the early summer of 1992, had been fraught with practical difficulties. It had been hard to find the right venue. Lydia shared with the 800 participants at the conference: 'Finally God led us to discover a building in a beautiful village in the mountains north of Prague. It wasn't luxurious, but it had a big hall where the students could play games.' Lydia had sent out invitations. But she had very little response, so she prayed, 'O Lord, is this camp really your will?' She then asked God for something very specific: 'Please, Lord, if you want this camp to go ahead, send me some applications tomorrow.' With suspense and excitement she waited for the next day's post. God answered her specific prayer. That next day, a few letters arrived. They were followed by many more. So many that, as she told her de Bron audience, 'I had to ask God to stop it!'

Yet this was not all that Lydia sought to achieve in these early days of SU's formation in the centre of Europe. She translated the Scripture Union's international aims, principles and basic beliefs into the Czech language, so that church leaders might have a real understanding of SU's ethos and range of ministries. Lydia began to explore the publishing of adult daily Bible reading notes. In 1993 I had written in an urgent prayer request sent out to friends and colleagues who were committed to praying regularly for SU's work in Central and Eastern Europe: 'In the Czech Republic we are going ahead with the publishing of adult Bible reading notes. For a year's printing and distribution we need up to £10,000 initial capital. This is a project which has been requested by one of the leading evangelical denominations; but they have no funds to contribute towards the costs.'

By this time, it was clear that Lydia was overburdened, working well outside the limits of a normal working week, frequently doing SU work at the weekends (Sundays as well as Saturdays). There was little quality time for family and the work at times appeared to give her no joy; there seemed little time for her to discover herself as a person known and loved by God. Her mother and sister were deeply concerned. I tried to identify the essential tasks with Lydia and to look for another person who could be the overall leader of SU in the Czech Republic.

Romania:
Beyond the Meanest Frontier

———e–o———

The Danube, scarcely blue for most of its 1,800 miles, from the Black Forest in southern Germany to the delta fanning out on the shores of the Black Sea, touches no fewer than ten countries. Robert Kaplan describes it as 'a river of hope, inspiration and cliché'.[1] It is a defining landmark in the heart of Eastern Europe, yet with a 'forgotten mouth' at the Eastern edge of Romania, staring out over the Black Sea.

As I attempt to draw word pictures of Romania in the late eighties and early nineties and especially at the epicentre of the changes in December 1989, I am acutely aware that I am in danger of oversimplifying. Robert Kaplan has written, 'The border between Hungary and Romania was for decades the meanest frontier crossing in Europe.'[2] Border police were rigorous and suspicious in their search of lorries and other vehicles. One day, we found ourselves waiting endlessly at a border crossing from Hungary into Romania. After several hours, when we were not prepared to pay a bribe to be whisked to the head of the queue – bribery was not on our list of options – we turned the car round and headed back to Budapest, deflated.

On that historic day, 17th December 1989, the Ceauşescu Regime collapsed and from Timişoara to Bucharest the revolution took shape. Eight days later, on Christmas Day, Elena and Nicolai Ceauşescu were speedily tried and convicted of genocide and sabotage and taken out to be shot by a firing squad. Individuals

---

[1] Robert D Kaplan. *Balkan Ghosts*. New York: St Martin's Press, 1993
[2] Robert D Kaplan. *Balkan Ghosts*. New York: St Martin's Press, 1993

experienced a mix of emotions: relief, hatred, fear, confusion. Some went to (the Orthodox) church, where they prayed. Mihai, a Romanian translator, said, 'Our minds swayed between Christ and Ceauşescu.'

Romania's revolution was by no means velvet and cleansing. There were many disturbing trends. Many independent newspapers, associations and political parties were founded, as the Romanian people realised their newfound freedom of speech and association. However the initial euphoria turned into vocal opposition to the new government, the Council for National Salvation. 1990 was punctuated by frequent, large anti-government demonstrations and numerous episodes of violence from a variety of quarters. In June of that year 20,000 miners arrived in Bucharest and terrorised the inhabitants. Many journalists and writers at that time left Romania.

Romania had been and still is naturally a beautiful country. Yet what I saw following the years of autocratic and repressive rule was not always picture-book! As we travelled by car through country and urban landscapes, we passed miles and miles of industrial pipes that 'uglified' the scenery, linked often and running towards industrial plants (Misha Glenny describes these as 'depressing industrial sculptures'[3]) belching black and obnoxious vapours over the fading green fields.

We left Budapest's Nyugati (West) Station, to travel east, on an early but sun-filled morning in May 1990. I was making my first (short) visit to Romania. I travelled with Marta Dobos, the daughter of our friends Agoston and Marta Dobos from Budapest, who in the seventies had arranged for their son Agoston along with Marta to attend an SU holiday activity in England. Marta had some friends in Oradea, my particular destination on that day. We took the train to the Hungarian–Romanian border, and then journeyed the few miles into the city of Oradea. Kaplan's acute perceptions fortunately were not mirrored in our experience that day; we walked from the train

---

[3] Misha Glenny. *The Rebirth of History*. London: Penguin, 1990

in Hungary across the border and caught a shabby bus into the city of Oradea.

I had arranged to meet Nelu Dan in Oradea. Dr Dan was well known to David and Valerie Hornsby of Romanian Aid Fund (David and Valerie would later work with SU, based in the capital, Bucharest, as sub-regional co-ordinators for SU in Eastern Europe); he was a dentist, living and working in Cluj, and with a passion for ministry among children. Valerie Hornsby had seen in him someone who might well help in the development of SU in Romania.

I found my way to the home of Nelu's brother-in-law, Nic Georghita, a leading Baptist pastor. While waiting for Nelu to arrive I was 'interrogated' by Pastor Nic. Rightly so! There were so many western Christians coming to Romania at that time, and particularly to Oradea, a border city, strong in Baptist allegiance and with several key Baptist leaders who had resisted the attempts of the Ceauşescu regime to 'domesticate' their ministry. Pastor Nic told me in no uncertain terms that it would not be possible for me to preach at his church that evening (that was never my intention) and quizzed me carefully as to what 'my mission' was, perhaps antici-pating my offering funding for church projects.

Nelu arrived, a little later than expected, and we had a pleasant and positive conversation about SU. He had both ideas and practical suggestions. But little was planned; moreover I had the impression that Nelu was someone sought after by several western and/or international mission agencies to help them get established. I was at pains to point out the subtle distinctive aspects of SU's approach and basic philosophy.

In the evening, Nelu returned to Cluj and I was taken to the Second Baptist church in Oradea (the largest Baptist congregation in the city and probably at that time, with 2,500 members, the largest Baptist church in the whole of Europe), where there were a sizeable number of worshippers in what was quite evidently an old and inadequate building. Shortage of seats meant that a significant number stood in the aisles and corridors during the whole two and a half hours – a norm for their evening mid-week service. Several leaders and visitors preached. Pastor Nic invited me to bring a brief greeting to the congregation and I was able to share something of SU's vision at that point. I looked around as the service came to an end and mused: could Scripture Union have a place in serving the churches in Romania?

The following morning, we picked up Marta at her friends' flat and Pastor Nic took us back to the border. We walked the short distance through border security and back into Hungary within ten or fifteen minutes. Hitching a lift to the nearest station, we caught the train back to Budapest.

What had been achieved? It was a beginning. There was potential. But, enthusiastic as he was to see Scripture Union as an effective tool for the churches in Romania, did Nelu Dan have the time, with an overfilled diary in his pocket and a multi-faceted range of interests and commitments on his heart, to bring to fruition a truly indigenous, autonomous and valued Romanian SU movement?

Teamwork:
Watford and Beyond

We had opened a small office in 1990, in a back room of St Luke's Church, Watford (where I had worshipped with Valerie and our family regularly since 1972). It was simple, functional and with limited space for three very second-hand desks. Yet it was warm and near the coffee-making facilities in the church. St Luke's were most generous in making this room available and let us have it for a peppercorn rent of £300 a year.

A friend of Nigel and Mary Sylvester, from nearby Chorleywood, built a computer for us. Cathie Buxton was appointed as a part-time secretary/administrator. Later Brenda Hilsden took over from Cathie, and after Brenda became ill, Janette Taylor was the person at the end of telephone calls, and much else besides. All three were strongly committed to the work. We regularly met together for prayer, catch-ups and planning; we talked through the issues which faced us, sometimes struggling with poor telephone communication with the staff and others in the Eastern European movements.

It would have been quite unrealistic to expect a part-time person to handle all that we did in setting up practical arrangements for the establishing of eight new SU movements in Eastern Europe. In addition to my wonderful PA/secretary, I had three faithful volunteers. Alison Houghton-Kral was a young Australian looking for opportunities to serve Christ in the UK. She was appointed to be a research assistant and, out of her experience of working with the Australian Treasury, put her hand to most things. She was a volunteer, although we helped with some of her basic living costs. She held the fort while I was travelling, although she also travelled

Brenda, Joy and Alison with my granddaughter Sarah looking on

*Twenty years later, Sarah (second left) helping at the children's club
at Siklós (Hungary)*

The East European Team 1996

occasionally with me and helped at one of the Polish student camps, where she met her future husband, also an Aussie.

Robert and Joy Simpson were my other greatly valued volunteers. Robert had retired from being MD of the local water company in Rickmansworth and came to oversee the financial operations, which involved regularly negotiating the transfer of funds to each of the new movements for salaries, expenses and the funding of projects, and drawing up draft budgets for the European Board to approve. Robert's wife, Joy, handled much of the publicity which was sent out to our prayer supporters. She further skilfully negotiated the movement of vital artwork for publications originally written in English but translated and published in most of the eight Central and Eastern European countries with fledgling SUs. This became quite a precise operation as one movement after another needed the same artwork around the same time of year.

This great team were really supportive, and, simply speaking, I could not have worked on my own without the immensely valuable and important contribution they all made.

Even when I was based at home in Watford, I was not always in the office. The LittWorld Conference at High Leigh in 1994 provided an opportunity to meet and dialogue with others involved in Eastern Europe. These events could be invaluable not only in the sense of strict promotion of what we were aiming to do, but in listening to and absorbing the wisdom and experience of 'fellow travellers'. There were a number of similar gatherings over the years. It was important to spend some time with the SU movements in the UK: meetings in London with SU staff, travelling to Scotland, speaking at promotion meetings, engaging with potential support-ers of SU's work in Eastern Europe. All these, along with writing reports and articles for magazines and Christian newspapers, were stimulating, as was my faltering progress in learning German. Crucially, meeting regularly with a group, mostly a group from church who were committed to supporting and praying for us, was a vital component to all that we sought to do in Eastern Europe.

My wife Valerie retired from teaching in 1991 but for some years before and after played a significant and immensely valuable part in much of my travel and in encouraging SU beginnings in Eastern Europe.

Nuisia Zachanovic was a young woman in her late teens when she travelled to England in the summer of 1983 for a few weeks to enjoy some exposure to Scripture Union in action. I had first met her in the winter of 1981, at a teenage camp in Bielice in Southern Poland, where she had brought several of her friends from school to engage with the good news of Jesus. Valerie and I were running a Scripture Union young people's camp in the beautiful setting of the village of Rougemont in August 1983, in the white highlands of French-speaking Switzerland. We had arranged for Nuisia to come to the camp; her life and testimony, we felt, would make a strong impact. Nuisia had left our home to travel to Austria and planned to return to us in Watford via our camp in Switzerland. She had only a 'limited stay' visa for Switzerland. We were driving to the camp from Bregenz in Austria and had arranged to meet Nuisia at the Austrian–Swiss border. We decided to conceal her passport at the back of our (British) passports, on the reasonable assumption that the checks were perfunctory and that they wouldn't examine the passports, waving us through into Switzerland. For Valerie this was not enough. As she looked carefully at Nuisia, Valerie concluded that Nuisia did not look 'British' – her hairstyle was the giveaway! So Valerie spent a few minutes out of sight of the border guards rearranging Nuisia's hair. No questions were asked and we drove calmly into Switzerland.

In the early nineties we were acutely aware of the need to fundraise for some of the new projects in Central and Eastern Europe. One of these was a family camp in Slovakia, run by the tiny Scripture Union movement in that country. There was a real need to provide a subsidy for families who were longing for a break but who simply couldn't afford even the modest fees. Valerie proposed that we invite several people in our parish to open their gardens on a Sunday afternoon and to invite their friends, church members and other people from the local community to go around all the five or six gardens, buying refreshments and making a gift towards the funding of the family camps in Slovakia. Valerie oversaw the plans and organised it brilliantly – with only one small hitch.

Naturally she wanted to include our own garden. A week before the event, our garden simply wasn't up to scratch. I offered to do some work on it. I spread some weed-killer on the lawn – a disaster, as the lawn turned black. Unimpressed but undaunted, Valerie conjured up an alternative strategy. We had an old and somewhat dilapidated World War II air-raid shelter in the garden. Valerie cleaned it out and found some old World War II newspapers in the attic, plus her father's ARP warden's tin helmet, his rattle and sundry other reminders of these bygone years. She bought a cassette of old World War II songs and arranged to play them down in the shelter. It worked and deflected attention away from the black lawn. Altogether we raised around £350 that afternoon and some families in Slovakia were able to go to the camp.

One of Valerie's concerns was to encourage the new SU movements in Eastern Europe to think creatively about how they might be involved in raising some funds, helping to contribute towards what the SU European Region and other Christian sources in the west provided. She discussed this with Nelu Dan from Romania at the SU international conference in de Bron in the late spring of 1992. He came up with the idea of getting Romanian Christians to make small models of traditional Romanian houses, selling these to Christians in the UK. Valerie saw this through, at least as an initial endeavour, and was responsible for selling a good number of these small 'gifts' in churches and at some promotion meetings in England. I don't recall how much we raised – a modest sum, I suppose – but it was a measure of Valerie's aim to encourage the 'receiving' movements to share the responsibility for helping to support and pay towards the costs of building a new SU movement.

Jean Lyon, an eighty-five-year-old Christian living in Dunblane, had been using her artistic gift for over ten years, painting some lovely Scottish scenes. Valerie and I travelled to Dunblane and viewed the paintings which Jean wanted to sell in order to raise funds for the SU work in Hungary. By this time, Valerie had been suffering from Alzheimer's for a few years, but she was able to concentrate on the paintings and helped to make the choices about which of them we would take back home to Watford. Our plan was to exhibit them in the front entrance of our new church building and to sell them – we agreed the prices that Jean suggested and later that year we raised over £400 for the work in Hungary, as Valerie stood by the paintings and encouraged different members and visitors to buy them!

Much earlier, in 1994, two meetings aiming to promote interest and prayer for the work in Eastern Europe were planned by the ebullient and active Paul Wilcox, SU's regional co-ordinator for the Midlands and East Anglia. One was held in Walsall, the other in Bury St Edmunds. I spoke at the Walsall event but Bury St Edmunds coincided with an important trip to Eastern Europe that I had to make at short notice. Robert and Joy Simpson, our stalwart volunteers in the Eastern Europe SU office in Watford, agreed to go with Valerie, who spoke about the work. Sometime after her death in 2009, I found her notes for the talk which she had planned to give at the Bury St Edmunds meeting. Written out in her very clear handwriting was her personal perspective on her husband's 'mad' change of life course. She concluded with an astute comparison: 'In Eastern Europe, there are now 12 Scripture Union staff workers in eight countries with a total population of 120 million. In England we have 200 SU staff workers for a population of 51 million – a rather different and revealing statistic.'

Throughout the twenty-five years from the winter of 1980, when I came back one evening from London to tell Valerie that I had been invited to go and help at a children's camp in Poland, she never failed in her support of all that I sought to do in Eastern Europe. On nine journeys to four different countries when we travelled together, she encouraged me and offered her practical wisdom in good times and less good times. At home, when I was travelling, she was alert, 'switched on' to my journeys and programmes. Over the years we both shared the privilege of welcoming into our home in Watford many from Eastern Europe – SU staff, volunteers, and their family members. All this enriched our lives, enabled us to build new friendships across cultures and encouraged us in our support and prayers for those in the 'new' SU movements.

*

Naturally there were days and weeks when I was visiting groups and individuals in Western Europe on behalf of IFES, as well as travelling regularly to Switzerland, France and Germany for SU European executive meetings. In my first full year I spent around twenty-one weeks travelling, mainly to Eastern Europe and the former Soviet republics. That was deemed too much by my mentors and seniors. I had to adjust, not only for my health but for my family's sake.

As I have written earlier, I had already travelled to parts of the former Soviet Union in late 1990 and early 1991. We considered ways of sharing the load. Danilo Gay, recently returned from SU French-speaking Canada (and who earlier had spent eleven years in

SU Bible engagement ministry in Zaire), expressed a strong interest in sharing the SU's developing ministry in Eastern Europe and the former Soviet Union. Danilo agreed to take on the challenge of the FSR and I would largely concentrate on Eastern and Central Europe. Danilo's fellow worker was Michael Rowe; Michael had been a much-valued researcher at the Keston Institute, which had become a leading voice on religious freedom in former communist countries, with an emphasis on the former Soviet Union. It made sense for me to free up time, as Danilo and Michael took over the reins of developing the links for SU and building trustful relationships with key leaders, all of which blossomed into authentic SU movements in different parts of the FSR.

In my role as IFES European consultant for high schools ministry, however, I travelled to Ukraine over ten days in February 1994. The focus of this visit was a conference organised by CCX, the growing student movement in the FSR. The conference would take place near Kiev, and there might be possibilities to explore developing high schools work. Around 400 students were present. Maiya Mikhalyuk, an SU worker and IFES student leader in Gorlovka, ran a programme of seminars with me. Maiya shared practical ideas and resources from her experience; I dealt with aims and objectives in a schools-based ministry. This experience was certainly worthwhile and also gave some opportunities to meet high schoolers as well as others who were interested in developing a ministry in high schools. Maiya's approach was distinctive, but perhaps with a preference for working with younger children.

During the early nineties IFES and SU had been discussing more generally how we might take forward work in high schools in the former Soviet republics. Across the globe, IFES and SU have had a history of close partnerships. In some countries, SU and IFES are joint movements. In Europe, we had an ongoing close association between IFES and SU movements, with a number of joint residential activities especially for high-school-aged students. Euroshare and other Europe-wide conferences for potential leaders have been organised in the UK and on the continent since the mid-seventies.

These focus on training young leaders for present and future opportunities.

It was the view of the leaders of the two movements that at this time SU should be seen as the 'senior partners' in schools ministry within the former Soviet Union, leaving IFES to develop ministry among students in tertiary education. Subsequent events and discussions led in that general direction with Grigori Stupak, the SU leader in Ukraine, taking the initiative in developing schools work.

Tito's Legacy:
Seams at Their Breaking Point

Misha Glenny's book *The Rebirth of History* (London: Penguin, 1990) contains a moving and illuminating chapter on Yugoslavia. He writes, 'Yugoslavia is the most seductive and beautiful country in central and southern Europe ... in its present form it is also the most hopeless, and, sadly, quite doomed ... in reality seven or eight countries, which eye one another with frustration, envy and resentment.' What then of Tito's fragile empire, a multinational state, which for many years resisted both Stalinism and consumer capitalism? What was life like for the Christian community during these years? The Christian theologian and writer Miroslav Volf writes of his experience in 1984, when serving in the Yugoslav military and summoned for a 'conversation' with Captain G, the security officer:

> Like the court in Franz Kafka's *The Trial*, my interrogators were going to pull out 'some profound guilt from somewhere where there was originally none at all.' I had engaged in religious propaganda on the [military] base – I must therefore be against socialism, which in Yugoslavia was linked officially to atheism. I had praised a Nazarene conscientious objector for acting according to his principles – I was therefore undermining the defence of our country. I had said something unkind about Tito – I was therefore an enemy of the people. I was married to an American and had studied in the West – I was therefore a spy ... I must be out to overthrow the regime. [But] the real issue ... was that the seams holding Yugoslavia together were at their breaking point.[1]

---

[1] Miroslav Volf. *The End of Memory*. Grand Rapids, Michigan: Eerdmans, 2006

From 1983, Joseph Riffert, based in Switzerland, had been quietly but effectively travelling on behalf of Scripture Union through Central and Eastern Europe. He met with church leaders, mostly Baptists, Pentecostals and Methodists, with a view to establishing an SU committee in Yugoslavia. There was a proposal to register SU in Osijek (in eastern Croatia). Later attempts were made to register SU in Belgrade (Serbia) but this was refused by the authorities. Ethnic tensions were a major factor in the failure to establish SU in Yugoslavia. Joseph made contact with Branco Lovrec, a Christian publisher based in Zagreb (Croatia); Daniel and Janet Berkovic, having earlier been in England studying, were back in Pula on the Istrian Peninsula by 1989; Lazar Stojsic, who subsequently published an SU 'Bible calendar', was a Pentecostal leader based in Belgrade and involved in Christian publishing. Would it be possible for them to work together to establish an SU ministry?

I first visited Yugoslavia in 1989. My links on this visit were mainly with IFES people: Stevan Madarjic and Giorgio Grij in Zagreb. Over that weekend they accompanied me on a two-day 620-mile trip by hired car, meeting Christians from a variety of denominations (Baptists, Church of God, Elim, Brethren, Methodists) at Osijek, Novi Sad, Kisač and Belgrade. In Osijek we talked to a young Baptist pastor who with his wife was involved in translating some children's Bible reading notes from SU Germany's *Guterstart* (I wasn't at all sure whether SU Germany knew about it, but at this point copyright permission was probably the least of the questions needing a solution). It was a whirlwind tour and at the end of it I was left breathless attempting to remember the names and perspectives of all the people I had met and all the discussions we had. Bible study outlines and other resources for high school students were high on the agenda of most whom we met. We engaged in the possibility of inviting some key young adults to see and experience camps and schools work in Western Europe later that year and/or in 1990.

Two years later I travelled on an extensive car journey with an SU colleague through Central Europe; Austria, Croatia and Hungary were our main destinations. Having journeyed from Austria via Italy on a pleasant, warm and sunny afternoon – the beaches around Trieste were covered in sun-soaked holidaymakers and local tourists! – we arrived in Pula, a lovely old town at the southern end of the Istrian Peninsula where Janet and Daniel Berkovic lived with their three children and where Daniel was the pastor of a small Pentecostal church. Spending time with them was an important step in beginning SU in Croatia. Janet, a no-nonsense English woman from Bolton, had worked earlier with IFES in the Netherlands and at an IFES conference had met Daniel, whom she later married. Janet knew SU well and had been using some of the *Learning Together* material in the Sunday school at the church in Pula. With acute foresight, she saw the benefits of translating this material and making it available to churches in Croatia, and she was excited about the prospect.

The following year, 1992, was the occasion of the SU international conference in de Bron, Netherlands, where around 700 people from SU movements around the world had gathered. A number of people, most of whom had a strong link with SU and a few of whom were already working for SU, paid or voluntarily, arrived by invitation from Central and Eastern Europe. The impact of the conference on them as well as their impact on the conference delegates was both significant and very moving.

Janet came to the conference, where we had some quite hardnosed discussions about how to proceed with *Learning Together* in Croatia. Janet had started to translate the material. Her desired goal was to produce the teaching material for three age levels. My able (voluntary) co-worker Alison Houghton was sceptical. Eventually, after some sharp discussion, we agreed on two age levels for the resources.

All this marked the small shoots of growth for SU in Croatia. The movement was registered later in 1992 and the following year I visited Zagreb, where Janet and Daniel were living with their family in Sveta Nedelja, a village on the outskirts of the capital. Daniel had taken on the role of pastor in the local evangelical church.

The general conditions in Croatia were critical. They were faced with internal hyperinflation of around 30% a month. The cost of SU teaching magazines when they were first published in September 1992 was 500 dinars (3 DM); in March of the following year Janet had to charge 2,000 dinars (value 2 DM). On the other hand the cost of translation was lower.

Serbian military aspirations were strong and threatening. Croatia was still on a war footing, even though the official ceasefire had come into effect in January 1992, along with international recognition of the Republic of Croatia as a sovereign state. Much of Croatia had been devastated in the war, with huge damage to both economy and infrastructure, and 20,000 people had been killed. One in ten children at the local school in Janet and Daniel's village were refugees from other disputed areas of Croatia, alongside some Muslim children from Bosnia.

The front line in the war had not been far from Janet's village. Telephone communication and travel to other parts of Croatia was problematic. During the war, the situation for the Berkovic family had been potentially quite dangerous. There were frequent air raids. Daniel had witnessed sky battles. In one of the worst nights of the war the Berkovic family were in Zagreb, faced with sniper gunfire and heavy air raids.

Janet was teaching part-time in the local school where four refugee daughters between the ages of six and sixteen had witnessed their parents being butchered in front of them. Many children were severely disturbed with the scars of war. Consequentially there were tensions between Christians throughout (the former) Yugoslavia. Some Christians in the west writing about the war were in danger of giving an interpretation of events which was strongly questioned by many Croatian Christians. A western Christian writer had (mis?)quoted one Croatian Christian saying about his Serbian brother in Christ, 'He is the kind of man who would carry bombs in one hand and prayers in the other; he needs to be converted.' All this was most damaging and in many respects deeply misleading. Yet at the same time there was a huge need and opportunity for Christian teaching with children and young people. I wrote in my report of this (1993) visit:

> The SU teaching magazines have been widely accepted in the (protestant) churches and Sunday schools. At school, children receive credits for religious education even though they are receiving this in Sunday school. The Sunday school teachers submit a report to the school … this meets the RE requirement for the protestant children who are not numerous enough to qualify for official protestant teaching at school. Some Catholics are also using this material, even though the catholic hierarchy has not yet given its imprimatur.

Janet worked hard to ensure that *Learning Together* could be accepted by Catholic educationists. She had some good reviews and an article in one of the Catholic magazines. Would there be a break-through into the Catholic market?

Janet, thoughtfully, had published the material undated so that she could continue to sell the booklets. Yet it was evident that we needed another person to extend SU work in Croatia. Janet was working for SU part-time, teaching in the local primary school in her remaining hours; she only had time to edit the Sunday school materials. She was not able to travel to churches in Croatia to promote *Learning the Bible Together* (the English translation of the Croatian name for this resource). She would have liked to begin with children's Bible reading material, introducing the distinctive SU approach. But another person would be needed to promote any further Bible-related material.

However, it was necessary to take account of what else was happening in respect of Christian publishing in Croatia. Duhovna Stvarnost, a Christian publishing house of which Branco Lovrec was director, had been distributing *Our Daily Bread*, a free adult daily Bible reading guide, now printing 20,000 copies. We would certainly be crazy to begin with adult Bible reading notes! Never-theless, the need for follow-up material in the wake of the Billy Graham Satellite Mission might lead to the possibility of translating one of SU's follow-up Bible reading guides from English … could

The 'dream' of a residential centre for SU Croatia, in Severin, 1999

Janet showing some of the early teaching materials

we co-operate with the newly formed Croatian Bible Society in this, perhaps? Especially if Daniel, Janet's husband, became the director of the Bible Society!

By 1994, when I next visited Croatia for six days, the city of Zagreb looked deceptively western. The controversial Benetton advertisement was well displayed; Croatians seemed to have no problems with something that showed a dead Croat soldier's bloodstained battle dress to the rest of the world. The area around Zagreb appeared unaffected by the war in Bosnia, in spite of the presence of significant numbers of refugees as well as UN personnel.

Church life seemed quite (but not hopelessly) fragmented. There was a good and reasonably united group of younger Christian leaders who came together from time to time, seemingly ignoring the 'flying visits' from the president of the Croatia Evangelical Alliance, a person of great ability and vision and with statesmanlike qualities. This situation was mirrored in other Eastern European countries, with key Christian leaders of necessity having to travel globally, but at the same time possibly losing touch with the realities in their home country.

On the positive side, there were some good interdenominational initiatives; a Christian poetry and music society was meeting regularly with attendances around 200. The Christian IFES student movement STEP had just held their first national conference with 150 present. Duhovna Stvarnost seemed to be flourishing not only as a publishing house but increasingly as a relief agency. SU Croatia was gaining an excellent reputation, mainly due to Janet's sustained efforts to give it a high-quality profile through the continued publishing of the teaching resources – with an excellent team involved. Yet volunteering was not easy for many; given the dire economic situation, most expected to be paid for what they did. A second worker, who would enable Janet to push on with new ideas and projects, was not yet on the horizon.

During this visit I spent some time with Drazen Glavas, the STEP leader in Croatia. Some high school students were already involved and had attended the student conference. But something like $150–200 a month would be needed for a full-time high schools worker and it became clear that this was not yet the major priority for the student movement in Croatia. Drazen was already frustrated by the lack of financial resources for the development of student ministries. Janet, too, found that coping with the ever-increasing amount of paperwork was draining her energy.

Standing back from their daily routines, I sought to analyse the development of Christian work in our small and fragile SU movements as critical, with the need for at least two people to work in tandem – even where one or both were working part-time. But in the beginnings of our ministry in Central and Eastern Europe, this seemed an unattainable immediate goal. At the same time, Janet had a good link with Ruth Lihovsky in Novi Sad (Serbia), who was part of a small group of five or six people enthusiastic about SU material and methods. Janet had already started putting children's Bible readings into a Croatian Christian children's monthly magazine: seven days of notes, and texts for the rest of the month. It was a modest but crucial beginning, given the limitations on Janet's time.

During these days, there was an opportunity to meet a Christian couple from Slovenia. The potential SU constituency there would be tiny, with fewer than 3,000 Protestants, many of whom were Lutherans. The husband, Daniel, invited me to visit him in Novo Mesto. Was this a straw in the wind, or whistling in the dark? Above all, what was God's plan?

I met up with Janet in England around Christmas 1994, but I returned to Croatia in March of 1995. In August 1994, I was assisting with a European high schools conference in Hungary. During a break in the conference, I travelled to Nagykanizsa in southern Hungary to meet Anica Kerep, a Croatian volunteer who was ready to join the Croatian SU staff team. By March the following year, Anica had joined the SU staff in Croatia. She was part-time, but had been able to travel to speak about SU in several churches in Croatia. She prepared the text for the first three months' children's Bible reading notes based on the English *Quest* notes. Anica, married with three children, had set up a 'work station' at home, adjacent to her husband's print room. She perceived her work outside her home responsibilities as a wife and mother as being 'normal' and as a calling for her. She was highly regarded by others, who saw her as a very gifted and able person. She combined all this with part-time work in an institution for mentally disabled people; she studied by extension in the theological faculty in Osijek. Truly a gifted and highly versatile committed believer!

By my 1995 visit SU Croatia had the makings of an excellent committee: people with a variety of skills and an understanding of SU, prepared to invest time and energy in the growth of this ministry. I wrote at the time, 'Potentially one of the best SU committees in Eastern Europe endorsing the practice of not going in at the beginning by trying to install a committee prematurely.' I had debated this principle long and hard with a number of my European SU colleagues. The first issue of the children's Bible reading notes was published in May of that year. I wrote, 'We now have a credible base from which to launch these notes.'

This visit had been a short one – twenty-eight hours! But it was most encouraging to see how the movement was being rooted in giftedness and clear objectives, with dedicated people.

I made two more brief visits to Croatia. In June 1997, it was again a flying visit to spend some time with the staff (Anica and Janet) and to travel to Osijek for the celebrations at the Osijek Theological School. These 'connections' were usually valuable; over the years I spent time on a number of occasions at events around Central and Eastern Europe where the value of my presence was not easily measured in concrete terms, yet I felt that visibility and openings, gently seeking opportunities to speak informally to different people, church leaders, potential SU supporters, had long-term value for the development of our SU movements.

My final visit to Croatia was in 1999, on a lightning trip from Budapest and back. I had returned to meet Janet and to visit Severin na Kupi, seventy-five minutes' drive from the Berkovic home in

Sveta Nedelja, and where SU Croatia had acquired a house on the edge of the village. Weather-wise it was a very soggy day, and we walked round with umbrellas and clad in wellies and kagouls. I saw this house as having great potential for training and evangelism among children and young people. I was no longer travelling to Croatia nor directly involved, but over the next few years, it took shape with the help of further funding, work camps, and a great deal of hard work on the part of the Croatian SU staff and volunteers. By March the following year, Janet wrote:

> Exciting project of house and ground (4–5 acres) which need to be prepared for children and young people. The first stage of the building extension work has been completed and the next stage just starting ... includes work on the electrics, heating and water. There will be sleeping accommodation for up to 36. An SU holiday/work party, with around 18 young people coming to work on the grounds.

One nineteen-year-old volunteer who had lost her mother earlier in the year, and her father four years before, spent most of the summer volunteering at Severin, where she learnt to cook and look after the house, take responsibility for herself and others, rise to the challenges and overcome dependence on others. She said, 'My best friend and I celebrated our birthdays in Severin ... in the evening, when everybody else had left, we felt God's presence specially with us. We prayed, cried, laughed all at the same time. We gave all that we have to Christ again.'

In 2002, SU were able to purchase a brand new Ford Transit nine-seater. They also purchased the 'hole' next to the house and cleared the site so that they could make a space for a sand volleyball court, amphitheatre, cable ride and sledge route. There were an increasing number of Catholic participants on camps. At SU Croatia's tenth birthday party, many of the children and young people brought their parents and siblings. There were several first-time conversions and other steps forward as SU Croatia began to experience the vision of an ongoing, year-round ministry bearing fruit. During the autumn of 2002 they planned to run seven weekends followed by a winter sports camp. Over the next few years, funds were raised for the further development of the residential centre. It was to prove an invaluable asset for the growth of SU's ministries in Croatia during the early years of the twenty-first century.

A fun game at the SU campsite in Severin, 2016

Yugoslavia:
Bosnian Coffee, Serbian Milk, Croatian Sugar

───⌐∽───

Lazar Stojsic had been in touch with SU for some years, the fruit of Joseph Riffert's quiet persistence. Lazar attended the international conference in de Bron (Netherlands) in May 1992 and joined with others from the newly freed countries from the communist bloc, in a wonderful celebration. As Michael Hews has written, 'Russia, Belarus, the three Baltic republics, seven countries in eastern Europe and Korea were all represented for the first time ... a remarkable answer to the specific prayers at the final meeting at the previous Conference in Harare in 1985, when the iron curtain had still been in place and Koreans had been refused visas.'[1]

In 1993, SU was registered in Yugoslavia/Serbia and an SU council established in Belgrade. Naturally the Balkans war overshadowed efforts to develop SU in the early nineties in Yugoslavia.

I had planned to visit Belgrade, following a meeting with Lazar at de Bron. Visas were not easy to obtain; travel was complicated and potentially hazardous against the background of the overall international situation. UN sanctions were firmly in place. But by June 1994, five years after I first travelled to Belgrade, the situation had eased. A few weeks before my visit, Stevan Kopcok, a member of the SU council in Serbia and pastor of the Church of God in Belgrade, had attended the SU European council in Fusch, and Nina

---

[1] Michael Hews. A Tale of Two Visions: *The Story of Scripture Union Worldwide.* Scripture Union: 2001

Djordjovic, a young Baptist from Novi Sad, had been involved at an SU training seminar at the same venue

I was met a few minutes before midnight, at the functional but drab Belgrade rail station, after a seven-hour journey from Budapest. Stevan and his friend Zeljko took me to Zeljko's and Gina's apartment, where I would stay for five days. They were welcoming hosts and made me feel very much at home.

The general atmosphere in Belgrade appeared deceptively normal. In spite of the sanctions, most people living in Belgrade were able to obtain the basic necessities of life; the shops were well stocked. Petrol was available, but not at the pumps – only on the street corners, from 'dodgy dealers' selling it in plastic bottles at around 3 DM (£1.25) a litre. The 'black' economy was endemic. Hungarians were travelling with full tanks to Yugoslavia, where they would siphon it out to sell it to the Yugoslavs. Crime rates were soaring. Two Christian workers had both had their vehicles stolen in the past few weeks. After a long period of hyperinflation, the currency rates had stabilised. Zeljko showed me a pile of dinar notes, with denominations of up to twelve figures, absolutely worthless and now superseded by newer and cleaner notes. I brought some of the 'worthless' old notes back home and used them occasionally in children's talks at church!

Church life in Belgrade appeared healthy and encouraging. There was some real evidence of growth, with many becoming Christians, especially young people. Sunday morning found me preaching at the Church of God (Pentecostal). The service was held in the city equivalent of a village community hall and had a genuine local and neighbourly feel about it. In a modest-sized congregation, the mainly young worshippers were informally dressed. After the service had ended, it was quite moving to meet a Bosnian (Muslim background) who served me with coffee, a Bosnian Croat (Catholic) who offered me milk, and a Bosnian Serb (Orthodox) who offered me sugar. All three of these young people were refugees from Sarajevo and had come to faith in Christ in Belgrade. The much larger Assembles of God (also Pentecostal) church where I preached in the evening, with a congregation of around 400, had a different atmosphere. The congregation were mostly formally and well dressed, in a refurbished church building well appointed with marble trimmings! Both of these centres for worship were vibrant fellowships.

On the previous day (Saturday) SU Serbia had held their general assembly. Dr Alexander Birish, the SU president, had been due to lecture at the Baptist Bible Institute and was unable to attend. Most of those attending came from Belgrade and from a spread of churches; four came from Novi Sad, including Ruth and Nina with whom I had had earlier links. I was invited to speak on SU's aims and working principles. These had been set out in an attractively produced booklet by the SU international council; by 1994 most of the 'new' movements in Central and Eastern Europe had translated this key statement into their own languages. Some good discussion followed with positive and practical questions. I recommended that those present work out what they saw as priorities for SU Serbia.

A small working group was formed; they decided to publish an annual Bible reading card, and the Serbian version of *Learning Together* (more easily translated from the Croatian version – which some in Serbia were already using). It was important, if the material was to be advocated widely, for it to be published in Cyrillic script. Additionally they advocated a training programme for potential camp leaders, so that they could develop a camps ministry. At the meeting people were invited to become members of Scripture Union, for which they were charged ten Deutschmarks!

Melita Vidovic (the wife of Dane, the IFES staff worker) was unable to come to the meeting. I spoke to her by telephone; she would come with six high school students to Budapest in the summer for the European high schools conference. Melita made some helpful comments about how SU might develop and offer practical help. Melita became SU Serbia chairperson in 2008, and she still holds that position today.

This was my last 'official' visit to Serbia. I wrote in my notes:

The quality and commitment of many of the young adults I spoke to during that Sunday was impressive. We cannot expect to develop strong SU movements in the 'new' countries of Europe, only with the assistance of 'experienced' people who are actually too busy and already over-committed. We have to win over younger people, young adults who are fired up to do mission for Jesus, and with time and energy to give … involvement in camps work could provide a platform for this … I urge the established SU movements in Western Europe to be available through their experienced staff to share the vision with young people in Serbia.

A year or so later, I invited two people from our 'Education in Churches' department in SU England & Wales to spend a weekend in Belgrade, teaching at a specially SU-organised conference for those working with children and young people in the context of both church and school. I applied for their visas in good time. Yet some weeks later there was still no response from the Yugoslav embassy in London. A few days before they were due to go I phoned our friends in Belgrade, who assured me that they wouldn't need visas. I hurriedly retrieved their passports from the embassy and they flew out to Budapest and then went by train to Belgrade. But, along with three Hari Krishna devotees from the Netherlands, they were refused entry and had to return to Budapest (I took a risk; they had to face the border guards!). Back at the rail station in Budapest they telephoned me at 6.30 on the Saturday morning: 'What do we do now?' My response was to suggest they have a relaxing weekend in Budapest before catching the return flight on Monday morning! Not everything appeared to work smoothly and successfully every time. The Serbian conference participants were disappointed but not at all fazed by the non-arrival of the two British speakers. They contacted a Christian child psychologist to do the main lectures at a few hours' notice and had a highly stimulating conference. Maybe I was too ready to send the 'experts' in from the west, when God had another plan.

Olga Dega was appointed as the first staff member in 1996. Olga was from Vršac, north-east of Belgrade. I had met her first at my last official SU European conference in 1996 (we met for a second time in 2000, when Valerie and I were invited to the SU European conference). For some years we kept in touch as I produced a regular (English-language) prayer and news bulletin about the work of SU in Eastern Europe.

In the summer of 2010, I travelled to Bulgaria to share in an international SU teen games. Olga was the leader of the Serbian group of young people. She 'rescued' me when I fell into a mountain stream just before I baptised Kaja, one of the young Polish team leaders, in a mountain lake. But I have more to write about this intriguing and sometimes hilarious short episode in my travels in the Balkans ...

In the early years of the new century, SU Serbia developed into a small but vibrant movement with a number of innovative approaches. Training their volunteer camp leaders in conflict resolution was an essential component of their programme in preparation for summer residential activities. Working with marginalised children and young people became an important part of reaching out to needy communities in the aftermath of war and

One of many SU Serbia activities

The Serbian team in Bulgaria at Teen Games 2010

deprivation. Their camps and schools programmes were imagina-
tive and colourful, capturing the interest and involvement of many
young people on the margins of church and Christian life. Olga
wrote in 2002, 'Thank God for 11 new volunteers, young people
open to SU activities and methods. We will have many activities in
the autumn: teens conference and the Bible reading clubs. We will
begin a [new] art competition "Strive" in October and we are
planning a "children at risk" training course in November with 50
participants from different churches.'

In the late autumn of 2010 and travelling from Hungary, I spent a
few days in Serbia and shared in a local primary school visit with
Olga. A small group of children were sharing in an after-school
session on 'the care of God's creation'. We began with a 'litter pick'
and afterwards planted new shrubs around the entrance to the
school in an endeavour to enhance the immediate environment. I

then spoke to the children about why and how we should care for God's world.

My last visit to Serbia was in 2012 when Olga invited me to speak at the annual general meeting of SU Serbia. The majority attending the meeting were young and enthusiastic volunteers who participated with a commitment and flair that was so deeply refreshing. On the following day I preached at two churches in the area, where there was real acceptance of what SU Serbia were seeking to do.

Olga wrote in mid-summer 2014:

Thank God for the books: 'Big Bible Challenge' and E100 for adults in the Serbian language, which are here now. Many readers will have opportunity to meet God every day through those books. Please pray that we accomplish our goal to reach many children in the churches, schools, camps and Christian clubs with this great book. Please pray for the cooperation with Bible Societies from five countries in the Balkans. Pray for the publishing E100 for adults and the start with the Bible groups in Christian churches around the Balkans. Pray for young SU volunteers who have been involved through being key persons in this project. Thank God for the SU teen conference. It has been a big event for youth every spring since 2006. It is a great privilege to spend time in the local church, be hosted in the homes of members and visit historical places in the city. Pray for the thirteen summer camps. Pray for our teams and cooperation with the local churches and the Christian organizations. Pray for new volunteers, especially to be open to learn, and to serve children and youth. Please pray that God would use them to present His Good News in the right way.

'You Are the Answer to Our Prayers'

—— ❧ ——

In the summer of 1996, Erzsebet Komlosi, who had joined the staff of SU Hungary earlier that year to pioneer work with schools and camps, ran a highly successful fortnight's children's holiday club. Over the subsequent years a growing number of holiday Bible clubs were held in the summer months, and up to thirty English-speaking young and older people shared a wonderful opportunity of getting involved in mission with needy Hungarian children. They were joined by increasing numbers of Hungarian volunteers who helped with translation and in many other practical ways. Derek Hobson's painstaking work on the Bible teaching programmes, with careful translations into Hungarian, were an important element in the programmes.

Over a period of four years, Andy Slatter, a young Tearfund accountant, led the team from the UK with his own inimitable style and flair. In the summer of 1998, I was travelling with Andy and the others in a 'bendy' bus to Pécel on the southern outskirts of Budapest. Dawn had just broken; we were due at the club at 7.30am, to set up and to welcome the children. Preparation in the previous thirty-six hours, since we had arrived at Budapest's Ferihegy airport on Saturday afternoon, had been inevitably brief; Andy conducted the final stages of it, standing in the gangway as the bus lurched round corners and as the rest of us quickly absorbed our respective responsibilities, sitting together on the back seats!

Around that time, I wrote in a short article for SU England's *Daily Bread*:

'You are the answer to our prayers,' the quiet spoken Erzsebet Komlosi shared, as the team met in the Scripture Union office, above

113

Kalvin Square in the heart of Budapest. For the month of July, twenty four volunteers came to Hungary, to share the good news of Jesus with children in eight separate church based missions, scattered throughout Hungary. This was the vision of Erzsebet, the Hungarian SU schools worker, and this was the third consecutive year in which churches had invited SU to get involved in working with children. During June we had witnessed the amazing coming together of the team, when it had seemed that there simply would not be sufficient people to help. David Blair had phoned Erzsebet, at the beginning of May, to pray for a miracle! Meanwhile Spring Harvest SU team members were alerted to the need, and many responded at the eleventh hour.

At Pécel, on the outskirts of Budapest, Sharon Mullen, a twenty year old care worker from Glasgow, told the children on the third day of the club, 'When I was eight I was invited to ask Jesus into my life but I was afraid it might change me. Would I wake up in the morning with green hair? I was told I could be born again, but I didn't want to start again being a baby!' Sharon went on to share how Jesus brought her new life and a new relationship as she discovered him as her best friend. Agi, a fifteen year old, came because her younger sister had been attracted to the club the previous year. By the third day, Agi was already beginning to respond and, in front of all the others in the discussion group, she said she knew she needed a relationship with Jesus. Following last year's club both her parents and another sister had started to attend church regularly, through seeing for themselves at the 'presentation' at the end of camp, what it meant to be a Christian. Building relationships with the children at the club was at the heart of the work, but was by no means easy. Some of the children knew some English; most of the British team knew one or two Hungarian words and phrases, at best. Yet Helen, a student from Durham on the team for the first time, recalls, 'Before going I thought language would be a real barrier, but it wasn't – it's amazing how much of a conversation you can have without words. The kids loved teaching me Hungarian and I loved learning it with them. During the breaks it was really interesting to see that it was possible to teach Bible stories through interpreters.'

One of the translators, Nikki, an eighteen year old high school student from Budapest, like many of the others, translated patiently and modelled Jesus to the children. Nikki spent much time in the first week just ensuring that Diana, a blind eight year old, was involved in all of the activities. Days began early at eight o'clock with Bible teaching based on Jesus' meeting with five people after his resurrection. Some children had already arrived by 7.30am! Then followed a kaleidoscope of activities – action songs, English conversation lessons, games, quizzes, plus a special daily fun challenge. Work sheets, which had been carefully translated at the last minute, were used during the discussion times, and craft projects reinforced the teaching.

At the end of the week, Jamie, who had previously helped at Spring Harvest children's events, said: 'I wasn't feeling particularly confident before going to Hungary. I knew I had to get to know people in a short space of time, but in the end I found it a good basis for me to be used in God's service.' Mark, another new team member, commented: 'I had to rely on God as this was very new to me, but I felt that God used me.' The church leaders were thrilled by the week's experience:

The 1999 holiday club at Pécel

Team members from the UK departing Heathrow

In the next year, in the church, we would like to continue what you have already done this week. We are thankful to God that you could tell the children that Jesus is alive. We would like you to organise a similar holiday club next year here in Mor not only for the children but also for the teenagers' wrote one of the ministers of the churches where we worked. Meanwhile in her mind and heart, Erzsebet plans even more clubs for the following year!

Over the next few years I continued to get involved mainly through recruiting young leaders in the UK who went to Hungary for a week or more in the summer to help run the clubs.

In 2001, Erzsebet Komlosi took over as the 'leading SU staff worker' in Hungary. In March of the following year, the SU Hungary board resigned and the future of the movement was thrown into uncertainty. Without a governing body, the movement could not function and there was a real threat of closure. Erzsebet set about finding new people to join the board. It took a few months to find the right people. She wrote:

The good people, who would qualify for the job were very busy, over-committed already. Yet, this crisis had its own benefits. It made

116

me realise once more how much we need to rely on God for everything. By our own strength we can do nothing – but with Him we can
do everything. With a handful of committed people, we were praying
for suitable new members. God has answered our prayer: within a
short time six people said yes, and finally four of them have become
Board members. We have an excellent group of dedicated people
who have a heart for God's work and for everything He wants to do
through SU here. So we are grateful to God for His answer, indeed!

In 2003, the volunteer team running the holiday Bible clubs based
the morning Bible teaching for the children on 'Desert Detectives',
an exciting SU programme for holiday clubs. Accurate and skilful
translation of this material required dedicated translators from the
SU movement in Hungary. A year earlier SU had run ten activities
in the summer, eight of which were English-language holiday Bible
clubs. At the teenage camps several young people expressed their
desire to follow Jesus. *YOYO*, a series of outlines for youth groups,
was translated and published. In the Budapest office it received
much positive feedback from pastors and youth leaders. For many
people this was their first encounter with SU.

Erzsebet faced the demanding task of keeping SU Hungary
'afloat' and wrote, 'Our total expenditure for this year is around
26,500 GBP. The central support we get from SU Europe is around
6600 GBP. Most of our core projects are self-supporting e.g. camps,
Bible reading notes and publishing, but it is very hard to find
money to cover salaries and normal running costs.'

In November 2003, SU Hungary celebrated its tenth anniversary
as a fully registered organisation. Valerie and I were invited to
attend an inspiring meeting, held in the Scottish mission church (St
Columba's) in Vorosmarty Street, a five-minute walk from the
'House of Terror' at 60 Andrassy Útca – a tourist attraction now, but
chillingly reminiscent of bygone years when Marxist terror was
very real. It was thrilling to see over a hundred supporters of SU
gathered on that day, and to witness the growth and development
of SU over the years.

A snippet from a prayer bulletin I wrote in retirement and sent to those who were committed to praying for the growth of SU in the former Warsaw Pact countries: 'Pray for continued and financially stable growth and for sustained efforts to reach children and young people in Hungary with the good news of Jesus Christ.' Also in 2003, St Luke's, Watford, generously agreed to contribute some ongoing support to assist in regular salary payments and to provide for a much-needed computer and printer.

In the summer of 2002 Neil Potts, a young graduate from Caerphilly who had had his first taste of working in a team with the holiday clubs programme, was making plans to go out to Hungary for at least twelve months, particularly to support SU work there and to help in the follow-up of the children's holiday clubs. Earlier in 2001 Andy Oatridge, also a member of the UK holiday clubs team, had devoted up to twelve months to assisting the work of SU Hungary and had established a teenage camp based at Kecskemét.

Erzsebet's visit to the UK in May 2004 enabled her to meet some churches and supporters of SU, and to share some of the stories. In the autumn of that year, Chris and Louise Harling went out to Hungary to work alongside Erzsebet and the team. Louise had first joined the children's club team in 2002. During her second year at the clubs, in July 2003, she became quite ill; her condition was quite serious, and as events quickly unfolded a Hungarian surgeon performed an emergency operation. Chris by this time had gone out to Hungary to be with Louise. After Louise's recovery, they were able to return to the UK together. In September of the following year, Chris and Louise came back to Hungary for a period of twelve months, to work as volunteers with SU.

Louise was mainly involved in some of the weekly clubs based in schools, as well as the preparation for the holiday clubs. Chris was more involved in 'background' work: admin for the British team coming in the summer, as well as helping Erzsebet in building strategy. He was a wonderfully clear-headed thinker and his input was greatly appreciated. They were both much loved and valued. In subsequent years, Chris continued to visit in the summer. In 2009, when I started to go out to Hungary again in July to help with the children's work, he was such a help to me as I planned to visit clubs some distance from Budapest on my own. He organised my travel, took me to the coach station and arranged my overnight stays. In 2010, Chris continued to help Andy Oatridge, who had set up through the 'Acorn Trust' a series of camps for teenagers. There was close co-operation with SU; some of the camps were run in tandem. But by 2012 Chris had become very ill and was unable to get further involved.

Valerie and I last visited SU Hungary together, in the autumn of 2006, to celebrate the opening of new offices in the shadow of the historic Calvinist church close to the centre of Budapest. Much had been achieved; much was yet to be done. A part-time 'camps' co-ordinator had been appointed (later, towards the end of 2007, the committee took the brave step of appointing a full-time person to this important and exciting new role). Erzsebet was in the midst of preparing for the translation and launch of *Christianity Explored* (an eight-week course to be used by churches to help adults who want to investigate Christian basics) and increasing number of volunteers were being recruited from both Hungary and the UK to assist with the growing programme of camps and clubs.

By 2009 I was able to take a more active interest again in the SU's ministry in Hungary. Tamás Daxner had been appointed in February of the previous year as programme co-ordinator. His main responsibility was facilitating the camping and holiday programmes. But additionally he maintained the website – an appealing and attractive resource to strengthen the reach of SU

Holiday clubs in full swing in Hungary

Hungary beyond the national office in the centre of Budapest. At the same time more and more churches in Hungary were using *Christianity Explored*; a day conference in June of 2008 attracted over 150 Christian leaders.

For six summers (2009 to 2014), I travelled to Hungary to help with Frontline Hungary, a growing number of children's holiday clubs, run in different locations. These had been a key part of SU's overall ministry since 1997 as we continued to recruit people from the UK (and elsewhere) who could help the Hungarian teams at the clubs. Native English speakers assisted in leading some conversational English groups each day of the week-long, non-residential holiday clubs, as well as helping in the Bible teaching and with a variety of practical activities during the day.

Following Chris and Louise Harling's one year's working with SU in Hungary, Steven Jemmett from New Zealand joined the team as a volunteer and engaged in running some school-based Bible clubs over a period of four years. Steven returned to New Zealand in October 2013 with his Hungarian wife, Lilla. Tamás Daxner took on additional responsibilities for the promotion of SU resources and, from March to September that year and the following year, was joined by Gabor Keleti, whose task was to help organise the summer children's clubs.

Christianity Explored was translated and published by SU Hungary. This led to new horizons for the movement and gave new opportunities for strong links with churches. But fruit from this initiative was to be found in changed lives...

'Jesus Christ gave me a new heart, I am saved! I belong to the Lord now, I have found my place!' ... 'At the beginning we asked questions fearfully, but slowly we felt encouraged to ask. We cried and laughed together. In the middle of the course I realized Someone is missing from my life ... I asked the pastor's wife to meet with me: I confessed my sins and God saved me' ... 'As a result of the course we have grown in our faith, found answers to many of our questions, had a new desire to read the Bible more frequently, and been blessed by the new relationships we formed. So it was hard to say good-bye when the programme was over, but we want to continue to meet in Bible study groups. We are very grateful to the Lord that He made all this possible.'[1]

In October 2013 I wrote in a newsletter to friends in the UK who were committed to praying for SU in Hungary:

Christianity Explored is now published in a Youth edition. SU Hungary are publishing regular Bible reading notes for women and Emesi helps in the editing of these, working in the office two days a week. Ildiko, who has been the office manager for twelve years, has recently resigned and SU Hungary is in the process of appointing her successor. One of the biggest publishing projects is about to roll off the presses in Budapest: *The Big Bible Challenge*, a beautifully designed children's (8–12) book to help children understand God's story throughout the whole of Scripture, will be published in Hungary by Scripture Union within a few weeks.

Later in 2014, Kinga, the daughter of Bulcsú (the first chairman of SU Hungary), took on the responsibility of office manager for a year; by September 2015 Kristina Borko had become the editor of the women's Bible reading notes.

Recruiting for the summer clubs became more challenging, year on year. Some, committed to this project, came back for several summers. For more than twelve years now, Moira Goddard, a children's worker in a church in Spalding, Lincolnshire, has been helping at the clubs and advising on all the aspects of the programme. Alison and Robert Nelson were able to recruit some younger people from their church in Edinburgh. I even managed to persuade two of my own family to join the team in 2013 – my daughter Anastasia and my granddaughter Sarah. Other friends and former colleagues helped to find those willing to come. Yet with up to fifteen clubs in one year, we struggled to meet the need.

---

[1] Scripture Union Hungary website (http://www.suhungary.com), accessed 2015

In the nineties Scripture Union in England and Wales offered significant support with articles in their magazine about the growth and challenges of the work in Eastern Europe, and financially supported me as I travelled in Eastern Europe. A number of SU English staff encouraged and helped in many ways, not least those who were able to travel and speak, train, advise. In the last fifteen years, however, SU in the UK have taken on new international responsibilities. Their national office team is smaller, and while they have always been prepared to look after much of the administration for Frontline Hungary, increasingly they have felt unable to advocate and promote this valuable project. It remains to be seen, with the advent of a new SU international 'community-based' structure, how this might strengthen and help to support not only SU Hungary but also a number of the smaller SU movements based in Central and Eastern Europe.

In January 2016 SU Hungary shared the following:

We have decided to give our website a total make-over, so we are busy working on it with some professional help. The aim is that it would be more user-friendly than the current one, compatible with mobile phones and tablets, complete with a 'proper' web-shop. Please pray, that by the time you read this it would be fully functional!

We have grown accustomed to changes in personnel in the last 2 years! The latest is that our camp-coordinator, Tamás Daxner's future has become uncertain with us, for family reasons. We are grateful if you pray for him and also for us, that God's guidance would be evident concerning whether he has to go or he is able to stay.

We are thankful to the Lord for our Board, for their enthusiasm and support. Please pray that we would continue to grow and work together pulling in the same direction as we seek to build God's kingdom through our SU work in our country.

Romania:
Not Level Enough for a Portable Easel

⸺ℰ∽⸺

In July 1990 I made a second short visit to Romania, accompanied by my Hungarian friend Bulcsú Széll. With his links in Transylvania Bulcsú took me to meet Hungarians living in Romania, of whom there were around 2 million. In 1989, it was in Timişoara in the Banat, a western frontier region of Romania where apparently the tensions between Hungarians and Romanians were less severe than in Transylvania, where the Revd László Tőkés, pastor of the (Hungarian) Reformed church in Timişoara, helped ignite the spark of revolution by his persistent preaching against the harsh communist regime and its policies under the iron fist of Nicolae Ceauşescu. When the authorities sought to move Tőkés into internal exile, both Romanians and Hungarians joined in the street protests in Timişoara which led, through a chain of events, to the eventual execution of Ceauşescu ten days later. Sadly, by the following year, one journalist wrote of a conversation with a Romanian Orthodox priest in which the priest said, 'The people still lack faith; they are suspicious of Laszlo Tokes because he is Hungarian. Tokes is a hero but no one will say a kind word about him. The truth is in our souls. But we are still afraid to speak it. We are a religious people but we have become a spiritually disfigured people.'[1]

We packed Bulcsú's small car on a hot summer's morning, with innumerable 'comfort supplies' for those we anticipated visiting. Our first stop was Oradea, the large city adjacent to the Hungarian border in north-west Romania where, later in the decade, the

---

[1] Robert D Kaplan. *Balkan Ghosts*. New York: St Martin's Press, 1993

Christian Emmanuel University would be established by Paul Negrut, a leading Romanian Baptist. My only link on this visit was with Sandor Fazakas, from the Hungarian Reformed church in Oradea. Sandor had links with SU Scotland and was particularly interested in youth evangelism, but he was leaving soon for a nine-month stay in Scotland on a scholarship. He would return in April 1991.

This and subsequent visits to Hungarian communities in Romania uncovered what became an unresolved set of questions in my experience of travelling in Eastern Europe. Historically there were sizeable Hungarian minorities in Slovakia, Ukraine, northern Yugoslavia and Romania. Throughout my travels in Eastern Europe, I had always made attempts to discover the needs of such communities (which also included a small remnant of German Lutherans in central Romania). Understandably, the new national SU movements in Eastern Europe, with severely limited resources, felt that they should focus their energies on the dominant language group in any one country. Their financial resources were tiny in comparison to older and more established SU movements in the west; they had to prioritise and choose what seemed to them the best way forward.

From Oradea we travelled east to the city of Cluj. En route, we tried to contact Benjamin Papp, a young man training for the ministry of the (Hungarian-language) Reformed church in Romania, and attending the International Christian College in Glasgow. However, Ben, who had begun translating some material from *Learning Together* (the English-language Sunday school teaching material), was not at home. Having arrived in Cluj, we stayed overnight with a family, sharing our personal testimonies with them and leaving some Christian literature, Bibles and food in at least one home. Our hosts were concerned about the safety of our vehicle and eventually found a neighbour who secured it behind a locked gate in their drive.

We had planned to travel further east to Târgu-Mure? to meet Monica and Laszlo Szabo, but neither was at home when I phoned;

I planned to meet them on a subsequent visit, but in spite of leaving a message, there was no further contact. So we journeyed further south to Aiud, where we spent a short time with the pastor of a small Reformed church congregation. Leaving some Bibles and other Christian literature we moved on to Arad, not so far from the border with Hungary. In trying to locate the flat of Marinella Damien and Jorza Viorica, we were perplexed that the street name was nowhere to be seen. We asked a passer-by; he agreed that we were indeed in the correct street but as he looked at the street name plate, he realised that the authorities had changed the name of the street only earlier that day (a Sunday)!

We spent some time with the two women, who were both engaged in children's ministry in the Baptist church in Arad – where there were no fewer than twelve separate Baptist congregations. Following a useful discussion about the need for Christian literature, we gave them some SU teaching magazines and some SU holiday club material. These were faithful women who had a real heart for ministry among children and young people. One of them shared with us that a few years earlier, during the communist rule, she was travelling to a (secret) children's camp when on the train she realised that she was being followed by a member of the Securitate. She quickly left the train, returned to her home city and began her journey again later the same day!

Finally, before driving back to Budapest late in the evening, we visited Rudolf Edward and his wife, who were friends and contacts of Bulcsú, and there we left Bibles, other Christian literature and some food supplies.

These had been an illuminating and rather exhausting two days. Most of our links were with Hungarian families and pastors. However, I sensed that one of the two Romanian women in Arad had real potential to be an SU staff member in Romania – perhaps our first! Later, I discovered she was likely to go to the USA permanently. Before, during and after the changes in 1989 in Eastern Europe, many well-taught and gifted Christians left their home country and few returned. The other woman was planning to be in

England later in the year for training in work with the mentally disabled. While she was not a strong leader, she had written after our visit to express her enthusiasm for SU and for the French-language materials I had sent her.

In August of the same year (1990) Margaret Old, leader of the Education in Churches department at SU London, travelled to Romania at the invitation of Nelu Dan to lead a training week for Sunday school teachers, at a beautifully located but quite basic chalet in the Carpathian Mountains near 'Red Lake'. Judith Copley and Ronalyn Reidy travelled with Margaret mainly to give support in the programme geared for teaching English in small groups – and were assisted by a team from International Messengers who had turned up unexpectedly! Likewise, the anticipated forty-five Sunday school teachers suddenly became seventy-one on arrival. The tinned meat generously donated by Romanian Aid Fund (which at that time was headed up by David and Valerie Hornsby) provided satisfying meals, but left Nelu with the problem of finding food for a following week's camp for twelve-to-sixteen-year-olds!

The interpreter arrived partway through Margaret's second session. The weather was kind and without rain; they were able to conduct many of the sessions on the hillside, though, as Margaret commented, 'after 12 noon [when the heat made it impossible to hold sessions seated at the tables outside the chalets] everyone climbed the hillside to the shade cast by the edge of the forest. [However] it was not easy to find a place level enough for a portable easel. I learned to stand still while leading a session: a false step could have led to me falling down the hillside.'

Following Margaret's visit, she noted in her report:

Baptist church buildings are [often] crowded and consist of one room ... good approaches to the teaching of children and young people are difficult for two reasons. The first is the lack of what we may regard as basic equipment. Large sheets or rolls of paper are unobtainable ... so are felt tip pens, sellotape, glue, pipe cleaners, yoghurt pots and blu-tack. Training needs to be done with materials that are available.

Second, while those present [at the conference] were extremely interested in the 'Learning Together' range and very hungry for ideas, they know that children are all too frequently bored with 'traditional' approaches. But new ways will be blocked unless there are changed attitudes among churches and congregations.

Margaret wrote about the problems that the Romanian Christian would be facing:

All the different strands of Christian sub-cultures and of the sects and other world faiths are beginning to flow in – we witnessed a Bahai public meeting in the town square in Cluj. Romanian Christians are going to need a great deal of wisdom and discernment to sort out what is a biblically-based alternative to what they already know, and what is not ... Nelu Dan is very concerned to have a Scripture Union national movement in Romania because he recognises the strong Biblical base we have ... He has dreams of a Scripture Union book-shop, perhaps at Cluj Railway station.

In October of the same year (1990) I made a further visit to Romania. This was seven days out of three weeks of travel – the longest set of journeys I made in all my years of travelling to Eastern Europe and the former Soviet republics. I left St Petersburg after breakfast, taken to the airport from the Intourist Hotel in a private coach – I was the sole passenger! Changing airports in Moscow was straightforward and by early evening, Aeroflot touched down in Bucharest.

By late 1990, Rodica Magdas was back in Romania, living with her parents. Rodica had studied in Switzerland at the Emmaus Bible Institute and had met several of my Swiss SU colleagues. She had shown interest in Scripture Union's resources – especially for young children (she was by training a primary school teacher) – as well as SU's approaches to working with children. For this visit to Romania, I had made some (not entirely well-defined) plans to meet Nelu and Rodica as well as other people who had expressed some interest in what SU might develop in that country.

Rodica and Nelu

John in Bucharest

The airport was unwelcoming, the arrival hall cavernous, draughty and bleak. After processing through customs, I looked carefully at the hundreds waiting to see if any held my name up on a piece of cardboard or, even more hopefully, if I should recognise any of them. It seemed that no one was around to meet me. I waited thirty minutes. My 'host' may have been held up on the way to the airport. But I decided I had no option but to succumb to the most friendly-looking of an array of eager taxi drivers.

He took charge of my luggage and drove recklessly through the unknown urban sprawl to a hotel which looked pleasant enough. We waited patiently while the hotel reception checked on available rooms. Nothing as yet was available, but if I would like to wait they would see what they could do. Were they waiting for me to offer a financial incentive for them to find me a room? I was ready to stick it out and to see what happened. The hotel seemed modestly respectable, even though I hadn't seen anything beyond the front lobby. The taxi driver was waiting in the shadows. He came over to indicate that this hotel was not a good plan and that he would take me to a better place. In the end I slept an uncomfortable night at the Turist Hotel, which provided no food, nor any lampshades – just bare lightbulbs hanging from a high ceiling – although it did have beds, of course: three in my room. I ended up paying for a three-bedded room in order to stay the night in safety and security.

The following morning, having been directed to an adjacent hotel which appeared at least one star up from the Turist, significantly cleaner and better appointed, I was served an adequate breakfast. A taxi to the centre of the city and to the rail station. I had phoned Nelu to ask what I should do; he told me to travel to Braşov. Purchasing a ticket after a half-hour wait in a long queue was a gentle challenge but nothing out of the ordinary. The train took some hours to reach Braşov, crossing first an extensive plain before coming to an attractive range of mountains on the north side of which lay the city of Braşov.

I had been able to contact Rodica and she met me with her father, who drove me to the family home. I had first met Rodica at Guebwiller in eastern France, earlier in June at an SU European meeting. Danilo Gay, my Swiss colleague, who at this time was making some visits to Eastern Europe prior to taking on responsibility for the development of SU in the FSR, had also met Rodica. She had begun the task of translating *Explorateur*, French-language Bible reading notes for children, into Romanian. Progress was steady but slow. I suggested that Danilo visit her in the early part of 1991 to encourage her to continue and to discuss with her the best way of publishing the material. Danilo additionally might lead some seminars on Bible engagement in her region of Romania.

During my days staying with Rodica's family she introduced me to Rodica Hortopanu, a young woman with a sense of call to Christian ministry with children and young people. In six months' time, Rodica Hortopanu was planning to leave Braşov for a period of study at Wiedenest, a Bible school in Germany. Could the two Rodicas form a creative partnership in shaping a programme of resources and events which would draw children into the kingdom? Translating SU materials into Romanian would be a tough slog. Yet I sensed a curious reluctance on the part of Rodica Magdas to involve Rodica Hortopanu in SU ministry. Could Rodica Hortopanu translate youth materials? Her skill in German and English would be a considerable asset. Subsequently, she helped in the SU summer camps in 1993.

During my stay in Braşov I met John, who pastored several village churches; I preached at Baptist and Brethren churches locally. It was a natural expectation of the Protestant churches in this region that any western Christian visitor would be preaching on each and every occasion. Yet it would take time for 'outsiders' to be known and trusted: all part of the slow process of SU becoming credible and accepted in a very different and 'new' culture, which had in recent years undergone dramatic change, bringing consequent uncertainties in both church and nation.

Rodica Magdas explored several ideas for the future of SU, bringing Christian teachers together – although Nelu Dan had already told me of the formation of a Christian teachers' organisation in Romania. There was a curious diversity and independence of thinking and action in respect of a number of new Christian initiatives. I had discovered in my role of IFES high schools consultant in Europe, which gave me many links with national IFES student ministry co-ordinators, that students in each university aimed to start up a Christian student group quite independently. There seemed little desire for collaboration and co-ordination. Was this all part of the legacy of mistrust over forty years?

Notwithstanding Rodica's good local connections with churches and leaders, overall I felt that she would be very much on her own, perhaps a lone voice in a predominantly male environment. I strongly urged her to pull together a small group to work with her and to oversee her projects and ideas. Rodica was studying at the Emmaus Bible College in Switzerland for a further year and would not be free to begin working with SU until 1992.

The day before the Evangelical Alliance Romania conference was due to open in Bucharest, I set off in the opposite direction to spend some hours with Nelu in Cluj. Trains were badly maintained and on a particularly sharp lurch round one of innumerable bends, my (first-class) single seat collapsed. I was sprawled across the floor with books, Walkman and sandwiches on top of me! The seat had come away from its base and was rolling helplessly at my side. Other passengers rushed to my rescue, got me to my feet, brushed me down and restored the seat in its base as best they could. When the ticket collector appeared in the carriage, many of the other passengers got to their feet and remonstrated angrily with him, pointing to me sympathetically. I was quite moved by their concern even though I had damaged nothing other than my dignity! Perhaps I had done them a service in encouraging a move forward to better, cleaner and safer railways in Romania?

Nelu met me in the crowded Cluj railway station and took me to his home – a solitary, old and somewhat dilapidated house, standing amidst huge blocks of flats. Apparently Ceauşescu's government had ordered the demolition of all the older houses in the street, to be replaced by tall, faceless and functional blocks. All the houses except Nelu's had been bulldozed. He and his family were particularly attached to their quaint dwelling – was it an answer to prayer?

In the few hours I spent with Nelu, I caught the sense of his personal enthusiasm for Scripture Union's Sunday school training which Margaret Old had led earlier in the summer. Nelu would become an important voice in establishing SU in Romania over the coming years. He told me that he anticipated retiring from his dental practice sometime in the following year, so that, at the age of fifty-five, he would have time to develop SU alongside undertaking many other mission opportunities. At present he seemed overcommitted with his professional work as well as the work of the Christian Medical Fellowship and the Baptist children's work.

Nelu had worked hard at finding others to assist in the development of SU. I hoped that he was working in tandem with Rodica but even at this stage I was not at all sure. He had spoken to Viorica and Marinella, both of whom I had met earlier in the year in Arad. He was keen to involve a young couple, Mihai and Anca Suciu, whom I would meet in Bucharest and get to know better over the next few years. Nelu had approached them and they were prepared to consider being involved in the growth of SU in Romania. That they were based in Bucharest would be advantageous, especially as I had already been sensing that we might become just a local organisation in Braşov. Another of Nelu's many interests was in establishing Christian publishing, especially printed resources for children. But was it realistic for Nelu to imagine that he had the time to come to England for 'training' as he was proposing? I believe this was a genuine desire but he would put it in the mix with all the other aspirations and possibilities.

Nelu's married daughter spent a little time talking to me as she was particularly concerned that SU should spend time working in eastern Romania – perhaps she felt, as many did in Transylvania, that they were already flooded out by western missions!

Following a hurried meal and brief meeting with his wife and family, Nelu whisked me back to the railway station for the overnight train to Bucharest. I had assumed that he would accompany me on the train, but he still had many things to do before he could travel to the capital.

The overnight train journey was a further rich experience of Romanian culture. Six of us – all men – were squeezed into one compartment; none of the other five spoke any English as far as I could guess. Suddenly, one of them switched the lights off, having already pulled out all the seats to make makeshift beds, six across, head to toe. My shoes were off and under the 'bed' – so it was a challenge in the middle of the night to respond to a call of nature. I found when I got into the corridor that I had put two shoes on my feet, neither of which belonged to me!

The next morning, at an early hour, the train pulled into Bucharest where I was met by Christi Tepes. If only he had met me when I had first arrived in Bucharest from Moscow, I mused. Christi worked for Romanian television and was hopeful for opportunities to introduce good-quality Christian programmes and videos on the main Romanian channels. He expressed some real interest in audio-visual material about which he had read in the Scripture Union catalogue, with a view to subtitling for Romanian TV.

We shared breakfast with Anca and Mihai Suciu. They were in their early thirties, with a strong vision for work amongst children and young people; Anca was a kindergarten teacher and Mihai an engineer. Their 'dream' was to purchase a house in the mountains as a permanent campsite – might this fit in with SU's established experience of camping programmes based on a permanent site? Could they come to England in 1991 to get some exposure to SU in action? Their knowledge of English was limited, yet they had a mature and balanced view of the dangers of financial dependency on 'western' sources. Nelu knew them and thought highly of them. At this stage, I was beginning to see the possibilities of a small team who might, between them, help to pioneer and prioritise the development of SU in Romania.

That morning, I was taken by Christi and some others to the Palace Hall in the heart of Bucharest where the first congress of the

Romanian Evangelical Alliance was being held over the next three days (19th–21st October). Twelve months before this historic event, Nicolae Ceauşescu had stood in the same hall, before his last party congress. As the EA congress began, I listened to the Minister for Cults, who welcomed more than 2,000 delegates with words of assurance that religious freedom would be guaranteed to evangelicals. His tone was optimistic: 'Our office is not for supervision and limiting; we want to defend and help.' John Alexander, a poet and member of the government and a leader in the (Orthodox) Lord's Army, invited the whole assembly to stand and pray in memory of '1,133 young people who died last December, all of them Christian'. Jonathan Aitken, a British member of parliament, was one of a number of speakers. Another was Paul Negrut of the Second Baptist church in Oradea (claimed to be the largest church in Europe), where Ceauşescu, a short year earlier, had made a chilling statement – in effect, an order to his destroying agents: 'When I come back to Oradea I do not want to see this church building.' Yet Jesus' words rang out over centuries and cultures: 'I will build my church, and the gates of Hell will not overcome it.' Such had been the persistence and faithfulness of the persecuted church in Romania.

Paul Negrut had been presented with a plaque, 'Torch for Freedom', at a British Conservative Party conference, and had brought the plaque to present to the president of the newly formed Evangelical Alliance. The congress brought together the major 'players' from the different groups and denominations that constituted Romanian evangelicalism. Would it be a landmark for the renewal of Christian life and witness in Romania?

Yet there was still physical and material deprivation. People spent long hours in queues for even the most basic foodstuffs. The country's infrastructure – electricity and water supply, telephone, road and rail communication – was fractured. Many were angry and frustrated. Humanly speaking, as I wrote in my notes, it was difficult to see how they could recover.

At the end of my visit, I travelled back to Moscow. But a significant delay in the flight found me sitting in the terminal building for several hours. They had removed a major glass frontage 'for repairs' in this soulless and cavernous structure, with minimal creature comforts and a cold gale sweeping around our feet. A bland cheese roll was about all that was available to purchase. However, I struck up a friendship with a Jewish Russian businessman named Ivan who was waiting for the same flight. He was travelling on to St Petersburg and was pessimistic about getting back to the northern side of the river Neva and home that day; the bridges closed at midnight and we didn't leave Bucharest until mid-evening. We swapped addresses and telephone numbers. On a later visit I made to Moscow and St Petersburg in February 1991, he came to my rescue, as I had got hopelessly lost in the city, and Ivan took me back to his home where I met his family. He even drove me to the church the following morning!

*

During my visit to Romania for five days in mid-December 1991, I met with the 'proto' SU committee in Braşov, when they were in the process of registering as an association. Perhaps optimistically, they anticipated official recognition within twenty-eight days. The committee appointed Rodica (in her absence – she was still in Switzerland) as their first staff worker, although at this point it was unclear whether she would continue part-time as a teacher. The publication of the first edition of the children's notes was 'on the way', but without a firm date. The committee had no budget drawn up, even though they had a strong sense of becoming self-supporting. They planned to send Rodica, Nelu, Anca and Mihai to the de Bron SU international conference in June of the following year – a crucial opportunity to meet the SU international family and to be involved in the movement worldwide.

Anca and Mihai were a wonderful couple. Yet they faced pressures in their home, church and work life. Mihai was an editor, Anca a kindergarten teacher; both attended a school of journalism five nights, twenty hours a week. In church, Anca headed up the children's ministry and Mihai was youth leader. They shared a flat with their family, but hoped to move into their own flat eventually.

At this time there were no fewer than six Christian high schools in Romania. One man told me that he had eighty-three pupils in his (Baptist) high school, 20% of whom were from a non-Christian background. Yet some younger evangelicals were critical of this attempt to penetrate the prevailing secular culture. *Super Book*, a Christian programme for children, was being screened nightly on one of the two national TV channels.

Yet a darker side was all too evident in Bucharest's lonely streets. In my notebook, recording impressions of Romania and the bleakness of the capital Bucharest, with hungry children begging at the promptings of an adult in the shadows, I wrote:

The children fly, they cry,
From the black and subterranean maze below Victory Square
Where victory, alas, eludes the hungry, frozen, small pathetic face.
Their hats, worn on head some time ago, and now upturned to
    receive unwilling lei,
Are not filled with the gold of kings, but with a few ungrateful coins,
    worthless to most in an opulent age, but survival to them in this
    city of tears.
They sing a shrill tone to shout at the passive, their hurt, their anger,
    at a time of year another child is celebrated. But he too knew the
    pain of being ignored, rejected, shut out from the world of dreams.
Dread night, the child plods home through snow blackened by soot
    and hardened by foot,
Creates a slippery mountain to catch the old, the cold, the careless,
    the drunk.
What hope?

My final day brought an early start to catch the plane back to the UK. I talked with Mihai and Anca about the many possibilities, opportunities and pitfalls, before Mihai took me to the airport. The minutes ticked by as we patiently waited for a bus in the snow-covered suburbs of northern Bucharest. After some time Mihai

An SU youth camp in the mountains

spotted one and hailed it. It was workers' transport taking the men to the factory. But Mihai managed to persuade the driver to divert to Otopeni airport. I made the flight with minutes to spare.

By 1992, the SU committee in Romania had been formalised, and in November of that year I spent seven days there. Teenage material from the French material *Rendezvous* was being translated. They had published the first edition of *Exploratorul*, the Romanian version of the three months of French Bible reading material for children. This had been a long and complicated journey. The committee were disappointed that there were so many mistakes in *Exploratorul*. Although Nelu and Rodica had made corrections, the committee were not convinced that the printer had noted these corrections. A small matter, perhaps, but indicative that at this early stage, we were struggling with time and budgetary constraints.

Rodica felt very much alone. The committee members, although enthusiastic about the potential for SU, simply didn't have the time in their lives to make a significant contribution. Geographical distance added to the sense of isolation, especially for Rodica. She lived and worked in Braşov; Mihai, Anca and Ana lived in Bucharest; Nelu lived in Cluj. It was agreed that for the second issue of the children's notes, Rodica would supervise the translation and Mihai, the engineer with editorial experience, would also help.

But in all these possible options for SU Romania, questions of distribution, costs and pricing, print runs and so on had to be faced realistically. I noted at the time:

Basic food distribution outside Bucharest is haphazard to say the least. In Cluj, the population have recently gone through ten days without any bread supplies; even when bread is available, people have to queue for many hours to buy it. Moreover, salaries simply do not match rising prices. In this climate is it responsible and realistic for us to expect people to pay for Christian resources such as daily Bible reading notes? One possible solution would be to encourage twinning churches in Western Europe to purchase Christian materials for their Romanian twinned church. But even that idea begs many questions. To create such a system of twinning would take more resources than we have currently got access to; a more practical solution might be to ask for funding so that the printed materials could be highly subsidised and made available through Romanian churches.

I had to recognise that much of the country's infrastructure was in a poor state. Roads, even main highways, were simply not maintained; rail links were preferable, but trains were generally slow, and track poorly maintained. Rodica had a car but could not afford to run it. Our chairman, Nelu, had two vehicles, both off the road and with no immediate hope of repair.

It was my perception that most people felt a deep sense of hopelessness and anger. Poverty was stark and begging children in most of the large cities a constant reality; in all, not so different from third-world communities and nations. Parallel to all this was the reality that SU Romania remained fragile. Most active Christians were immersed in their church activity and in the business of personal survival. My sense was that we needed to find younger volunteers and optimistically, I wrote at that time, 'I believe that we are beginning to find them'.

In stark contrast, in the early nineties, much 'western' money, mainly from the other side of the Atlantic, was being poured into the building of very large and well-equipped churches, yet with a danger of creating false impressions in the intelligent and perceptive minds of Romanians outside the Christian community. Some Romanian Christians questioned the wisdom of this apparent desire to have large congregations and saw it as part of the 'Americanisation' of Romania and the Romanian Church, and with the tacit encouragement of some Romanian Christian leaders. Yet I realise that some will strongly disagree with this view, having participated in some major breakthroughs in the growth of at least some major Christian enterprises.

At the same time the style of church life seemed to some, especially younger Christians looking to different solutions, as legalistic and introverted, fearful of change and in some cases apprehensive of western control. They saw reflected in this a mentality of 'centralism', linked in some ways to the legacy of totalitarian rule, which in Christian terms had often led to a stifling of personal initiatives, replaced by the much safer demands made on worshippers spending many hours each week inside the four walls of the church building. Some adventurous younger Christians were at least questioning these traditions, challenging both the old traditions of evangelicalism and the superficiality of much western Christian influence. Their desire was to witness a more truly Romanian Christian transformation in all parts of society.

There were additional tensions where evangelical groups and congregations viewed the dominance of the Orthodox Church as an instrument of repression and, in extreme cases, persecution. In its turn the Orthodox Church saw itself as authentically Romanian and viewed evangelicals as cultic, a western 'import'. This overall mix seemed potentially destabilising for the fruitful and effective growth and influence of an authentic Christian voice in 'tomorrow's' Romania.

In autumn 1993, I wrote in my diary, 'I remain deeply concerned about the situation for Rodica and the future of SU work in Romania … there is little financial stability in the country; beyond Braşov and a local network of Brethren churches, there is little perception as to what SU is and what it might offer.' Rodica was giving serious consideration to returning to teaching; 'We live with capitalist prices but socialist salaries,' she had said. To buy a pair of shoes, a dress or a jacket would cost almost 50% of an average monthly salary. How did people survive in this almost impossible financial climate? Many had second or even third jobs. Some had invested in the dubious and controversial 'Caritas' Bank, whereby they hoped to gain eight times what they had invested after three months! A businessman at the airport laconically informed me, 'Over 1 million people in the end will lose all the money they have invested; only a few will make anything.' His judgement was that there would soon be riots on the streets of Cluj.

For all this, there were a number of positive signs. Rodica had run two SU camps in the summer, with fifty-five teenagers at the first, and thirty-five younger children at the second. Rodica Hortopanu, the younger woman whom I had met the previous year, was now studying at Wiedenest Bible School in Germany, and had ably assisted even though there were some tensions between the two women. By this time Rodica Magdas had also started with the translation of *C'est Vrai* (a children's Bible reading booklet), for which she was offered generous help by Claire-Lise de Benoit from SU Switzerland.

Constantin Alexandrescu had arrived in Braşov when Rodica's brother in law had driven me there from Otopeni airport. Constantin was living in Iaşi, a sizeable city in north-east Romania where he was a professor at the Agricultural Institute, teaching technical English, landscape gardening and forestry. His vision as a Christian was to work with his students in small group Bible studies and evangelism. He expressed genuine interest in being involved, sometime in the future, with SU Romania. He might even strengthen our fragile committee!

On that Saturday evening, and after Nelu had returned to Cluj, we went to the local church to speak to the youth group – but no one turned up, so we travelled to nearby Râşnov, where I spoke to a small group about the importance of Bible reading in the Christian life. The following morning (Sunday) I spoke at the local church and then was driven forty miles to lead the youth group at Făgăraş. The young people were eager and attentive as I used a brilliantly designed leaflet put together by my SU Swiss colleague Danilo Gay. I spoke again at the evening service in Făgăraş. Mr Cornea – an interesting person, intellectually sophisticated, not a 'conformist' perhaps, one who might find it difficult to fit into the typical Romanian church scene – had translated one of the SU French-language booklets for teens, *Rendezvous*.

The next day, Simona from Samuel (not her brother, father or husband but the name of a Christian printing house in Mediaş, a nearby town!) brought the final proofs of the second quarter of *Exploratorul*. Yet progress on this project was slow, laborious and fraught with a number of disappointments, and possibly in the end would result in a poor-quality production.

In the evening we travelled to Ghimbav where I spoke at yet another Brethren church. They were welcoming and open, yet, on reflection, I felt that Rodica and SU Romania needed to 'widen the door' into the different church groupings.

During the remaining two days of this visit to Braşov and before I set off again for Bucharest, we spent time planning future visits from SU people of Switzerland and Western Europe, and exploring a possible site for a camp for children and young people in the following year (1994).

In Bucharest, I met Mircea Pop and Lidia Tirziu, both young leaders of student groups at Bucharest University, who expressed some interest in developing a high schools ministry. In the evening I led a Bible study with twelve key student leaders, who were meeting together to plan a Christian programme for their small groups, sharing what was happening in the different faculties. Rodica had arranged for Frans van Dijk from SU Belgium, when he visited in November, to speak to the student group. It was encouraging to reflect on the number of people from Western Europe who in a variety of ways were prepared to visit, to speak, to advise, to help both in student ministry and in the development of Scripture Union.

The flat belonging to Mircea and his wife was available to me for the night, while they generously departed to stay with in-laws. Unfortunately I hadn't spotted an open window through which an army of mosquitos had entered with a readiness to bite! Just before I left for the airport to fly back to the UK, I managed to fit in a meeting with Mihai, one of the SU committee; it seemed so important that the people who were beginning to get involved in SU were kept on board, even when I was covered with red blisters!

In late August of the following year 120 Christians from different church backgrounds came together for the first ever SU family camp. I travelled to Romania in November of that year (1994) to assess progress with Rodica and the committee, but there were others I wanted to meet, in particular John Anderson, working with Romanian Angel Appeal (a charity established by the Beatles' wives). In the past twelve months Frans van Dijk (SU Belgium), Vicki Shaver (SU Scotland) and Jean Pierre Besse (SU Switzerland) had all travelled to Romania and given invaluable help to Rodica and Scripture Union there. This was vital resourcing of a young and fragile movement. But now I was keen to visit Iaşi and spend some time with Constantin and others.

Rodica was to resume teaching (twenty hours a week) soon after my visit in 1994. Her teaching post left her with some time to work for SU (which she also treated as a full-time appointment).

Generally, not much had changed in respect of the general economic, social and political scene in Romania. Fast food culture had arrived in Bucharest, but the burger price was high. There was some evidence of continuing pressure from the Orthodox Church, which had blocked (although only temporarily) some Evangelical Alliance sponsored television programmes. Christian youth leaders were expressing real concern about the lack of effective work among teenagers in the churches. A few predicted that the church was in danger of losing a whole generation of young people either to secular culture or to radically alternative church styles. The leader of the Crusader movement (now, in the twenty-first century, 'Urban Saints') in Romania, Liviu Cosmuc, was heading up a coalition of youth workers and was a dynamic influence for change in ministry to young people. Sadly SU Romania had not been able to work with this 'stream' thus far.

John Anderson took me to his church in Bucharest, where we met the pastor, Ote Bunaciu, and took part in the service. Ote's wife had given birth earlier in the week, but it was three or four days before Ote was allowed into the hospital to visit her and the baby. The state still seemed to control all the events surrounding the birth of a child, to the exclusion of the father. John and I sat meekly in a waiting area just inside the hospital while Ote was visiting his wife and child for the first time, but after a few minutes we were told very clearly and bluntly to get out! The only welcome 'visitor' was a stray dog.

All this gave me an opportunity to speak to John about a possible future role for him with SU Romania, for it was clear by this time that Rodica's role in developing SU in Romania would be limited.

Later, I was invited to speak to eighty students at the Baptist theological seminary. Helping future pastors and leaders of the church appeared to be invaluable in creating an awareness of SU and how it might help them, as pastors, in the future. In the evening of my second day in Bucharest, I was invited to the university student group, eighty or ninety strong, to speak and to meet Luxita, who had brought a number of high school students to our conference in Hungary earlier in the summer. Disappointingly there was little time to explore with her how we might begin to grow a high schools ministry in Romania and whether she might be involved in that.

John and I met Rodica in Braşov. Early on the following day we all travelled together on a six-hour rail journey to Iaşi, a city in the far north-east. Met by Constantin (whom I had first met one year before in Braşov), we spent an encouraging two days speaking at and visiting churches: not so difficult as they all began and ended at different times during the day, and even if we arrived late and left early it didn't seem to matter. Constantin and Alena, his wife, reflecting the lives of many busy people, were already heavily involved in ministry among students in Iaşi. But they were alert to the opportunities for SU and it would be good to involve them and others in Iaşi. Rodica would need to 'change gear' and travel much more widely if all this was to grow effectively. There had been many delays in the printing and publishing of SU material; it was not always clear why this was so.

I left for the UK two days after returning from Iaşi. While I was encouraged by our visit to Iaşi, my own sense was overall disappointment that we were simply not yet well established and known in Romania. The car journey back from Braşov to Otopeni airport was punctuated by a breakdown and a 'swapped' second car. We made it just in time for the flight. Was all this symbolic of how SU would need to develop and change, to be in time with God and his people in Romania?

John was fluent in Romanian and was willing to work for SU full-time from the beginning of 1995. Our hope was that Rodica might continue to work mainly in the area of translation, and on a contract basis.

Subsequently I travelled twice to Romania in March and April 1995 for two rather painful meetings. At the second meeting in late April, the members of the SU committee were voted out of office and SU was left hanging by a thread with John the only remaining 'officer' of the movement. The main issue was over the control of SU Romania. The Braşov-dominated committee wanted it to be based in Braşov and for them alone to determine the future of SU. This was neither an ideal nor a satisfactory solution, and the movement had to regroup at a later stage with a new committee and with John appointed as the leading staff member.

Rodica left SU and continued in full-time teaching. Over the next four or five years John focussed on developing an effective camps ministry with teens. Nelu was re-elected as the chair of the new committee. By 1998, John was organising and running three camps each summer, aiming to recruit young people for a number of different cities in Romania and reaching out to those who were not yet Christian. Over the first two or three years, John was involved in the training of twenty-five leaders for the camps plus five 'junior' leaders.

Nelu Dan corresponded with me following an SU European seminar in 1995, which I had planned in Budapest for staff and volunteers from the 'new' movements in Central and Eastern Europe. Unfortunately I was unable to travel, because of ill health. Nelu wrote, 'I am glad that you knew and recommended John Anderson to stay in our country and help. I perceive a real progress, and appreciate his faithfulness to God, his dedication in ministry, and with the spirit of collaboration with us Romanians, he unites us in the work.'

This was a most encouraging sign. On the one hand, from the European SU perspective, we were reluctant to appoint anyone other than nationals to leading roles in the new movements. Normally there would be a language problem. Further, it was not the policy of SU worldwide to send missionaries! However, we always had exceptions, since there were exceptional people called by God and sometimes exceptional circumstances that required a different approach. We had a leading staff member from England pioneering the SU ministry in Bulgaria for four years – we 'discovered' Helen Parry, already teaching in Bulgaria – and Janet Berkovic, living in Croatia and married to a Croatian pastor, led the movement there for a number of years. But in each case they were encouraged to look for a successor who was a national of the country concerned.

John was national co-ordinator of SU Romania for five years. During that time he worked closely with the newly formed committee, who were, by 2000, widely representative of churches and regions of Romania. With the help of David and Valerie Hornsby, John developed the literature resources. In 1999 new Bible reading notes for younger children were piloted based on the SU England *Snapshots* and titled *Clic!* Teenage notes were also being published by this time. In these months, a Romanian teenager wrote to John:

> I was very glad when I received your letter and the 2 Bible study notes. Each morning I read from the 'Oxigen' notes and it helps me very much. My younger sister reads 'Exploratorul'. I like very much the way the temptation is treated ... at the beginning it surprised me, but after that I liked it and have tried to apply it to my life ... I would like to be one of the SU volunteers. Please write to me what I must do to become a volunteer of SU Romania.

Into the twenty-first century, SU Romania continued to develop and grow. Alex Bruda and Ema Carstea, Romanian SU staff workers, worked together, making extensive links with key Christian leaders. The movement published four children's stories and two books for teens. They exceeded the sales limit for non-profit organisations and had to set up a limited company ...

By 2002 they began to print and promote a new modern series of Bible reading notes called *e-mail*. Many teens were, in their words, 'in an advanced stage of apathy', and they specifically asked for prayer that this project would meet a need and touch the lives of many young people.

Two years ago (in 2014) SU Romania wrote to ask, 'Please pray for our winter activities! This year we want to start the shoe box project again! Every volunteer collects presents from their friends, and at Christmas time we give them to children from poor areas in Romania.'

Now based in Timişoara, Cristi Maritan, the present leader of SU Romania, wrote in 2015:

> We are thankful for all that God has done for us in the last year and we are very excited about this new year and all the new challenges that come with it! This winter we want to have again a ski camp in a resort in Romania for SU volunteers and for teenagers, especially those who are not Christians. Please pray for wisdom and that we manage to organise everything well, for finances to be able to support those who can't afford to pay for a ski camp. Also pray for God's protection during the camp, that no accidents will happen and that young people get to know God during this camp. This year we hope that we will have our own office here in Timişoara, so pray that all the problems will be solved and we will finally be able to buy an apartment! We could really see God working until now and we know that He will continue to take care of SU Romania.

And one year later:

> As the New Year (2016) begins, we want to initiate a new project, to restart publishing. We want to publish devotionals, books and vacation Bible school materials. Please pray for wisdom to know what material is needed in Romania and also to find the necessary funds. It is a big project, but we know God will help us find the proper way to launch it.
>
> During the February winter holiday, we want to organise a ski camp. We are praying to find ski and snowboarding instructors that are willing to give up their vacation to teach others. Pray also that God will protect us and help us share His Word through this camp. Thank you for supporting us in prayer!

Czech Challenge,
Parachutes, and the Stocks

———ᘓ ᘔ———

In the early autumn of 1991, we organised a schools training weekend in the evangelical church at Tabor, in the south-west area of the Czech Republic. I took a small team, including Keith Judson, Brian Sedgwick and Alison Houghton, along with Gerry Parr, a friend of Keith's. The local pastor, Daniel Kaleta, and his gifted wife, Grazyna, committed to working with high school pupils, had arranged a good programme.

Out of that experience, and more generally travelling through Eastern Europe, Brian Sedgwick sensed God calling him to move to Prague and to begin a schools and camps work linked to SU in the Czech Republic. In 1993 Brian joined the staff team in Prague and began learning the Czech language. Brian explored opportunities for reaching teenagers at school. The 'Czech Challenge' camp, run by Ann Baker and linked closely to SU England's interest at that time in the growing work in Central and Eastern Europe, became one of Brian's early responsibilities.

By 1995, Brian wrote, 'The 3 year project which SU England had set up as a result of celebrating 100 years of camps ministry, is now complete. Are we, Biblická Jednota – the name of SU in Czech – ready to begin leading these camps and developing them as Czech camps rather than relying on the British group to continue running them for us?'

Even though at that time they only had a small number of Czech leaders, they felt it right to plan a youth leadership camp for the sixteen-plus age group and to follow that 'training camp' by engaging these young leaders in helping to run a camp for the twelve-to-fourteens. Thus twenty-five young Czech leaders came in the blazing heat of the Czech summer, to study the principles of Christian leadership and their practical application to camps work.

Brian was able to assist Lydia Trnkova in a number of practical ways and began making a number of contacts with young people in Prague, while continuing to teach English for fourteen hours a week. He began to build links with three or four schools in Prague and develop a programme initially in English.

One drawback for Brian at this stage was the struggle to become fluent in Czech. This was not easy for him, yet he persevered over the years. At times, the SU European board raised important and challenging questions as to Brian's longer-term goals and aspirations. Yet Brian stuck to his God-given calling, and twenty years later he continues to exercise a faithful and fruitful ministry with young people. Through camps, cafés and character building, his work is crucial in bringing many young people to the Lord and establishing a tried and trusted team of young leaders. Schools ministry has been hard going at times – entry and acceptance has not always been possible – but Brian has worked tirelessly to encourage the few Christian young people at school and has networked well with other Christian agencies.

On a visit to Prague in 2013 with Hilary (now my wife, and this was our honeymoon!), I was struck by a comment from a leading Protestant pastor. On the Sunday, we went to worship at the Free Brethren church at Soukenická, where Pavel Cerny, whom I had first met thirty years before in Kutná Hora, was now the pastor. He welcomed us warmly and arranged for a delightful man to translate for us. After the service and over coffee in the church hall, Pavel came to renew his personal friendship with me and, talking about Brian, paid tribute to his work with young people. He shared that Brian had faithfully stayed in the Czech Republic for twenty years and had got alongside young people, bringing many of them into a personal relationship with Jesus and going on to disciple and train them as Christian leaders. Sitting opposite us at coffee was Vera

Bernatzikova, who was introduced to SU with Lydia at the SU international conference in de Bron back in 1992.

Although Brian was not the leader of SU in the Czech Republic, his distinctive ministry has contributed to the rich diversity of what SU has been doing in this central European country. Nor was he the only person to come into SU in Prague in the early nineties from outside the country. Daniela Seitz, a young German, had been working with Operation Mobilisation in České Budějovice for two years before Brian's arrival. By this time Daniela was proficient in the Czech language and in 1995 she was working closely alongside Michaela Krejci, a young Czech believer gifted in working with children. Early in 1996 they were both invited to be responsible for the children's programme during a large Catholic Charismatic conference with over 200 people attending. They used *King's Club* material sent from SU England. Daniela wrote: 'The parents were grateful as well as the organisers of the conference; we were able to share about SU, but it was scary to speak Czech in front of 200.'

Subsequently they ran a summer camp for thirty children when Czech TV came to make a programme about a typical day at camp. Daniela wrote:

About a month ago, I bought an old parachute for just 300Kcs (£7.50). When they heard it was for children the small 'sport' airport gave it to me for a symbolic price. It was white, but I bought special colours made of silk – more expensive than the parachute! And then painted it myself on the balcony of the flat where I live. It looks beautiful and it's the only one on earth that looks like it. We have already used it three times – the children love it – it's something new here!

Daniela and Michaela spent some days in Watford with Valerie and me – where amongst other things we took them to Aldbury to taste an experience of the mediaeval stocks!

Michaela running a children's club

Brian arriving in Prague

One weakness in the new movement in the Czech Republic was the lack of an effective and supportive SU committee. In the early years of SU's work in the Czech Republic, Lydia worked very much on her own, from the bedroom of her home on the eastern outskirts of Prague. Her own family, her mother and her sister were personally supportive and helpful, but for some years we had no effective committee. In the mid-nineties an office was found in central Prague, small, cramped, but just about adequate.

Lydia Trnkova had achieved so much over the years, as she pioneered the SU movement in Czechoslovakia (and from 1993 the Czech Republic). The foundations had been well laid and the ministry of SU Czech Republic was increasingly known and valued in the churches.

Lydia left the staff in 1996, and Pavel Tuma, in retirement, worked in the office for some years as an office manager. SU adult Bible reading notes had been published for some years, initially by another publisher, under the direction of a young and dynamic editor, Zdenek Voitisek. However, most of the denominations were publishing their own notes, and it was difficult to break into the existing market. So the next step was to find another national leader, who would be free to travel through the country and advocate SU as a movement working with children, young people and families.

Today, Martin Hejl, the leader, has overall responsibility for a wide variety of activities: ski camps and a range of summer camps with crafts, sports and music alongside related leadership training; working with schools in Prague-West; involvement in evangelistic campaigns and 'movie' evangelistic clubs amongst young school pupils. For some years SU has organised a junior Bible knowledge championship. Remarkably, in recent years a team from SU in the Czech Republic have also been to Worthing in Sussex, assisting with the running of a holiday Bible club for children aged from five to thirteen.

Slovakia:
The Living Stones That Remain

Traces of the 'Soviet legacy' were not difficult to find in many parts of the former communist bloc. In another context someone has written, 'The Soviet legacy has also left its mark ... spiritual practices such as prayer and worship were repressed and set aside as useless and harmful, diverting people away from the real world. Religion was regarded as the main impediment ... to a classless socialist utopia.'[1] A motto displayed at a high school in Slovakia conveyed these chilling words: 'There will never be prosperity until the last remaining priest is struck down with the last remaining stone from the last remaining church.'[2]

Viola Fronkova had been a member of the Czechoslovak communist party, and became a Christian in 1969, while studying in Oxford, through a personal link with Professor Jim Houston and Northway Evangelical Church. Viola subsequently renounced her party membership and suffered as a consequence. After the changes in Eastern Europe, Viola wrote:

In Czechoslovakia and also in other eastern European countries, there are dear communist comrades who have lost their faith in communism and are trying now to understand the Bible. As a woman from the Slovak government recently told me: 'people are expecting now that somebody will call them to faith ... the changes in 1989 proved so clearly that a system with a built-in atheistic approach to life cannot work.'

---

[1] Joshua T Searle and Mykhailo N Cherenkov. *A Future and a Hope*. Eugene, Oregon: Wipf and Stock, 2014

[2] Cited in the *Keston News Service*

For Viola, Bible teaching and personal Bible reading were essentials. 'How much more now, in these years of freedom, should we offer this Word to those who have been denied it for so long?'

My first visit to Bratislava and Slovakia – still an integral part of Czechoslovakia at that time – was in early April 1990. Jim Hartley and I travelled by hired car from Frankfurt to Prague, Tábor and on to Bratislava, where we arrived in the dismal street lights to find our hotel.

Personal contacts were integral to building confidence in Scripture Union, especially with church leaders. The pastor of the Evangelical free church in Bratislava, Jan Novak, was a young man who, as we walked through the shopping centre the following morning, explained to me something of the background of their church life and witness while at the same time he was looking for bananas! It had been rumoured that a consignment of these much-sought-after fruits had arrived in the city.

Jan was interested in the Sunday school teacher's conference that we had discussed with Lydia and others in Prague. One of my immediate aims was to invite one or two from this part of Czecho-slovakia to join the European conference in Switzerland, later in the year.

On my next visit in late July I met again with Jan and also with Natalia, a member of his church, who was involved in children's ministry. I was accompanied on this trip by Richard Wallis, our bookshops manager in SU England. We drove from Munich via Amstetten, Vienna and Budapest; our second 'lap' took us to Romania – Oradea, Cluj, Arad, returning to Budapest and to Bratislava. The following morning we had to visit the police station, this time to extend our visa which was fast running out.

Jan Novak shared with me the new children's magazine *Duha* (meaning 'rainbow'), for which Natalia Luptakova was responsible. It was printed in the Slovak language, similar but different to the Czech language, and they had around a 4,000 print run. The magazine sold at five crowns (around twelve pence). It was attrac-tively produced and it seemed that they would be interested in inserting into *Duha* some SU material from our activity leaflets and teaching magazines. *Duha* was overseen by an editorial committee representing different churches.

One option open to us at this time would be to appoint Natalia as our first SU worker in this part of Czechoslovakia, working with the church and enabling her to develop SU ministries for children. Claire-Lise de Benoit (working with SU French-speaking Switzerland) and Janet Morgan (from SU England) were planning to visit Prague on the 13th October to lead a training conference on children's work. Would it be possible for them to add on Bratislava for an additional venue for a meeting with children's workers and Sunday school leaders? No definite answer came, as Jim and I had to move quickly on to Ostrava. Reaching Gliwice in Poland early the following day was essential, for another 'key' meeting. Unfinished business or waiting on God to make the future clear?

In September of that year I returned by rail to Bratislava. We confirmed Claire-Lise's and Janet's arrival in Bratislava for Sunday 14th October deliberately quite precisely: between ten and eleven in the morning. Such precision was not always normal! They would aim to have lunch with Natalia and explore her vision for the potential for SU work. Natalia was a trained engineer and professionally worked in design. I had calculated that we could pay her a reasonable full-time salary in SU, since we had already received substantial funds through the Women's World Day of Prayer that year, raised specifically for Christian work in Czechoslovakia. I thought in terms of two years, initially. However, I realised that in the medium or long term we would have to reckon with a significant rise in Czechoslovakian salaries.

Jan Novak raised concerns. How important was it for us that we propagate the SU name? My response was that we should see this project as a partnership but in the longer term we would want to move towards the establishment of an indigenous Czechoslovakian SU. Meanwhile, back to 'reality': we learnt that there was an acute shortage of paper, and the September issue of *Duha* had not yet been published. We completed the planning for the 14th October event.

The news that Janet and Claire-Lise would travel from Vienna to Bratislava and back by bus was good – faster this way than by train.

We met Viola, who by this time was working for the Central Institute of National Economic Research. She was eager to develop a ministry through both English-language and Slovak Bible reading materials, as well as SU teaching resources. Viola was a Lutheran and had close links with the theological seminary. That morning, she took me to the Lutheran church. Unfortunately, the service was over by the time we got there (I lost count, over the years, of the number of church services where we arrived late or at the end or even after they had gone home!). However, I met Pastor Muntag, who was the spiritual director of the Lutheran theological students' residence and who was interested in someone who might give practical training in youth ministry to the students. He wanted a month's training – I felt that was impractical, so I suggested an intensive week – but in the end, while it was a good idea, it didn't materialise. I continued to learn that good ideas don't always equate with God's plans.

Meanwhile it was clear to me that Jan Novak was carrying a huge load, given that the senior pastor of the Evangelical church in Cukrová was in Canada for some months. The number of western mission agencies arriving in Bratislava and especially at this church could well have overwhelmed him. This was not an isolated problem in the countries and churches of Central Europe.

My visits to and travels through Central and Eastern Europe in the first year were frequent, so I was again in Slovakia by November. Natalia had written a most constructive letter to me in early October. In essence, she would become an honorary member of SU and we agreed to buy a laser printer with money we might have used to pay her a salary. With her background in design and her gifts for working with children, the cartoon strips in the English children's Bible reading notes (*Quest*) attracted her. Little Fish books, children's stories published by SU England, would, she felt, meet a real need in Slovakia. And it seemed sensible to invite Natalia to come to England for up to ten days for some training, and to meet editors and others in publishing.

The early pioneers of SU Slovakia including Natalia, Viola and Alena

The 1993 Yellow Tent mission

Peter Kroslak, working at the university teaching English in the theological faculty, was introduced to me by Viola. Peter emphasised the importance of treating Slovakia as a separate nation. This was prophetic! Three years later came the division of the Czech Republic and Slovakia. Peter subsequently became the secretary of the Lutheran Church in Slovakia – a big challenge. At this critical time for SU, he was a helpful friend with many good ideas for SU work in Slovakia.

During this trip I also met the general bishop of the Lutheran Church in Slovakia, Pavel Jahorski. New to his post and in his seventies, he had been imprisoned for almost three years in the 1960s, by the communist authorities, for engaging in youth work. Now, he reflected a quiet spiritual authority rooted in his integrity and faithfulness when under persecution. The Lutheran Church, with 350,000 members (out of a total population of around 5 million), was the largest Protestant church in Slovakia. The bishop emphasised the importance of prioritising Christian resources for children.

We all met together at the main Lutheran church in Bratislava on the Sunday, where I was invited to preach. After the service, the four of us set off to Viola's flat for lunch. The bishop, who could speak no English, sat in the front of the car with me. Foolishly, I 'misread' the traffic lights. On some of the main roads the lights were switched to orange on Sundays. I assumed wrongly that I was on the main road; we narrowly missed a collision with another vehicle. There was silence in the car for fully ten seconds, after which Viola solemnly declared that 'the Lord spared brother bishop'!

Viola appeared ready at this stage to begin working with SU. In early 1991, I prepared a brief for those from SU Europe and England who would go to Czechoslovakia to share in training Sunday school teachers, in Bible teaching at pastors' conferences and in general encouragement in Prague, Tábor and Bratislava. It was over a period when the Eastern Europe office was set up in Watford. For some weeks I was travelling to Eastern Germany, the Soviet Union and Berlin for an IFES meeting with other high school leaders in

Europe. During the month of March 1991, I squeezed in a short visit to Czechoslovakia. I had limited time to spend with those who would travel on our behalf. But I was thankful to people such as Danilo Gay, Janet Morgan, Claire-Lise de Benoit and John Grayston who were ready to help in this way.

Natalia was to travel in the other direction and in March she spent ten days in our home and in London, meeting SU staff and absorbing some of the values of our movement. The Sunday school training course which Janet and Claire-Lise ran in Bratislava led to the planning of two further courses in East and West Slovakia in February and March of the same year. Many possibilities for the future growth of SU work in Slovakia were discussed. These were sifted, evaluated and, on more than one occasion, had to be put on the back burner, given the shortage of funds and the fact that people were not always available nor ready to begin with SU. There was some uncertainty about how Viola and Natalia would serve as SU staff. They both attended the international SU conference in de Bron, Netherlands, in June 1992. But increasingly Viola had felt it right to remain in her role in the Lutheran Church and to help and assist SU in an honorary capacity.

The formal division of Slovakia and the Czech Republic into two separate nations became a reality on the 1st January 1993.

By early 1994, Viola had decided to withdraw from active involvement in SU and to concentrate on her active and fulfilling post in the Lutheran Church. Nevertheless her wisdom in these early days was greatly valued and her willingness to explore options for development of SU was admirable.

Natalia worked closely with Najed (Hope Publishing), which had close links to her church, but by the beginning of 1992 she had made some progress in translating SU England's *Time for the Family* as a possible first publishing project of SU Slovakia. Later that year, I noted that progress was slow but both Natalia and Viola were active in the translation and it looked like it would be ready soon for publication. This reflected the heavy commitments of both women in other and important directions.

In that year a committee was formed, as representative as possible of the various churches. I read Natalia's translation of the Slovak SU constitution. I wrote in my notes, 'While some things in it are a little surprising, I do not feel that it is misleading!'

During these early days, I was always warmly welcomed into the homes of Natalia and Andre, Natalia's parents, and of Viola and her brother, occasionally sleeping in the kitchen in Viola's tiny flat. All this was invaluable for building good personal relations with those who it seemed had caught the vision for SU work in this country. At the same time the more formal aspects of building a new movement were shaping up. SU became registered in the early part of 1992 and an application to be accepted within the SU Europe structure as a non-autonomous movement was put forward.

Typical of the 'provisional' nature of growing SU in the former communist bloc, I wrote early in 1992, 'Viola was out of the city [Bratislava] during the days I was there. I left her a note to contact me when she comes to England in connection with her academic studies the following week. Apparently she has found a young person who may be willing to work for SU in the future. However I did not meet him. I propose returning for 3 days in early April to follow this up.' Subsequently, it transpired that this man was doing his military service and Viola was uncertain of when he would be available. Later that year, when Bohdan Hroban was discharged from the army, he carefully considered applying to work with SU, but decided against it and took up a post teaching in a secondary school.

Slavomir Jankovic, married to Diana, an English woman, was another person who was interested in working with SU during this period. His concern was to translate and make available teenage material. I sent him the current issue of the English teenage materials *AM/PM*. Diana was interested in being involved in schools work. But by September, I found that both Slavomir and Diana had felt God moving them in a different direction. This happened more than once and not only in Slovakia. It was disappointing and occasionally discouraging. However, in part, the reason lay in our (SU Europe's) inability to move quickly and make decisions. Of course there were a number of opportunities for able people to work with a growing number of western mission agencies, and we had to learn to accept this situation.

By mid-1993 Alena Lachova joined the staff in a part-time capacity. She helped Viola to prepare for the publication of *Time for the Family* and was responsible also for the financial part of this tiny but growing movement. Alena and her husband Lacho, who was also on the SU staff for a number of years from 1998, were active in the Apostolic (Pentecostal) church in Bratislava – this brought a good balance to the movement and to the committee. They had a plan to start two camps, but the detailed preparation and decision-making began too late and they had to abandon this idea.

In June 1993, on a fleeting visit, I was taken to the 'Yellow Tent mission' in a village some distance from Bratislava. I was introduced to the president of the Apostolic Church of Slovakia and, with not much time for preparation, I was invited to give the children's talk. The church was experiencing growth and it was important that we work with this and other churches.

Spending time cultivating my links with IFES people in Slovakia was a regular part of my travel schedule. Peter Synak, who became the first Slovakian leader of the student movement, responded enthusiastically to the opportunity for a high schools ministry. My brief to work with IFES in Europe for 25% of my time, and to assist the development of high schools work in Europe, was a natural complement to Scripture Union development.

Peter, remarkably, spent three days in July of '93 travelling with me to eastern Slovakia – almost as far as the Ukrainian border – in search of a suitable location to hold the IFES high schools conference the following year. We inspected fifteen locations, but in the end none proved really suitable for our purposes and the conference was held the following year in Hungary. We considered and prayed about the idea of buying a property in eastern Slovakia – but this also proved to be unrealistic. Now, more than twenty years on, and looking back on this and other similar plans and visions in the

1990s to build or buy a residential centre in Bulgaria and possibly in other countries, I am still uncertain about the wisdom of spending scarce financial resources on bricks and mortar. Yet I recognise that in other newer movements (e.g. Ukraine, Croatia, Tajikistan) they have gone down this route and found it has opened doors to new and exciting activities for younger and older people.

Significantly, this mini-tour of eastern Slovakia gave us the opportunity of meeting pastors and others and sharing the vision of SU and high schools work. On the way back to Bratislava we met with Milos Pastrnak, a thirty-year-old non-English-speaking Slovak, who lived in a small flat with his wife and five children. Milos was already working with high school students in his local area, Liptovský Hrádok near the High Tatras. We invited him to start officially with IFES Slovakia at the beginning of August 1993. His subsequent schools ministry was in a fairly restricted geographical area close to his home town.

Milos had a unique style in his approach to schools, was faithful and undertook a valuable ministry. Some Lutheran pastors were critical and this probably reflected subtle differences in theology and practice. It was not easy for me to communicate with Milos as he spoke no English or German. I spent a hot day in Bratislava. Peter was preoccupied with many things. His wife was unwell, though she courageously helped me interpret Milos's Slovak into English, for a time. Milos and I eventually went to a restaurant where we shared an amusing lunchtime trying to communicate and finally discovering that we both could speak a bit of French! Yet these were occasions when I felt vulnerable and ill-equipped. Why hadn't I taken time to learn at least the basics of one Slavic language?

In 1994, Chris Elston, who was living and working in South Croydon at the time (having returned from a year's teaching in East Africa), felt God was calling him to Slovakia. Chris began teaching in the Lutheran grammar school in Košice in eastern Slovakia. Natalia saw this as having real potential for starting *Quest* clubs, once the material for these became available. Milos and Peter concurred with my idea of helping to start English-language Bible study groups in the high schools. For Chris, language would be a challenge, at least in the beginning. Over the ensuing years, Chris, who had an 'informal' relationship with SU Slovakia, visited many churches in his area of Slovakia, introducing personal Bible reading and forming small groups for those who wanted to explore the Bible. The twenty-first century saw Chris develop links with churches in Moldova and in northern Serbia, always seeking to bring about personal transformation in the lives of those he met, taught and discipled.

Later in 1994, I made a brief visit to Bratislava. Stefan Markus, the father of Natalia and the SU chairperson, took me on a short Sunday-afternoon tour of the old centre in Bratislava. Stefan's academic background was in sound and vibration and in 1968 he worked on the Concorde project. Denys Mead from Southampton University met Stefan in 1967. Mead was an active member of Above Bar Church, where Stefan worshipped while spending a year working alongside him. Mead wrote:

> Dr Stefan Markus arrived from the Slovak Academy of Sciences in Bratislava when Czecho-Slovakia was vainly grasping for freedom from USSR. Stefan worked with me on the theory of heavily-damped sandwich plates for one year. As a committed Christian under Marxism, he could rise to no higher position in his Academy than a small-group leader, but when communist domination ended, the Academy staff elected him as their Director. Being fluent in several languages (especially in Hungarian) he was [later in the nineties] appointed in a final career change as Slovakia's Ambassador to Hungary. He was a remarkably humble and gifted man, and I feel privileged to have worked with him for over 30 years.

Stefan was an excellent chairperson of the new SU movement, and led the small but dedicated SU committee with grace and skill. He and his wife Drahomira (Dada for short) were the most welcoming and hospitable hosts when I stayed in their home from time to time. In the late nineties Valerie and I were to meet them again on a snowy day in Budapest, with a lunch at the Slovak embassy and a short but memorable conversation with Stefan, when he told us of his opportunities to reach small Slovak communities within the borders of Hungary and to offer them SU Bible reading resources.

In the early years, Natalia's vision was very much related to the opportunities for SU Slovakia to work with children and families. So they published one edition, translated into Slovak, of SU England's *Time for the Family*. Optimistically they had printed 5,000 copies, but sales were slow, as were the sales of the children's Bible reading notes translated from the English *Quest* notes. Nevertheless, there were other encouragements. Just over forty adults and children had come together in the summer for a first ever families camp/holiday with the theme 'love is not love until you give it away'. The follow-up plans were innovative, with a family Christmas Day, a one-day holiday club for children, and the beginnings of some school Bible clubs, where SU was able to introduce children's Bible reading notes in Slovak.

Slovakian Scripture Union family camps in the Tatras

The following year, following a brief stop-over in Bratislava, I travelled to Hungary at the same time that SU Slovakia were running a family day with the assistance of Bob Johnston, sports ministry director from SU Canada. The planned family camp was full!

In early 1996, over a weekend, I made my last visit to Slovakia before retirement in 1998. I had noted, 'SU Slovakia is a small but healthy movement … they are focussing on limited but achievable objectives, mainly in the area of families' ministry.' Natalia, who was bringing up a young family, was naturally limited in terms of both time and travel. Stefan, her father, as SU chair would travel later in the year to France for the SU Europe council meeting.

I recall travelling back in the train with Stefan to Switzerland, when we had a long conversation about SU in Europe, especially in the 'new' countries and in Russia. Stefan was from a free church background. We had a fascinating, albeit short, discussion about the way SU were working with some people from the Russian Orthodox Church. Given the recent history of compromise and accommodation evidenced among the Orthodox Church hierarchy, leading to the marginalisation and persecution of Pentecostal and Baptist communities, Stefan expressed some surprise.

Interestingly, Michael Bourdeaux, in the foreword to *A Future and a Hope*, refers to the practical concept of symphonia between church and state in Russia, adopted over a millennium before, in which the two work in concert, and writes: 'Since the collapse of communism, the symphonia has resounded with ever more glaring political orchestration.'[3] On the other hand it had become clear that many believers within the Orthodox tradition were ready for what SU was offering and were willing to get involved in helping to reach out to the vast majority of the nominally Orthodox.

By 1999, Natalia had become a paid (part-time) staff member of SU Slovakia. For almost nine years she had worked as a volunteer. Yet much had been accomplished. Alena and her husband, of

---

[3] Joshua T Searle and Mykhailo N Cherenkov. *A Future and a Hope*. Eugene, Oregon: Wipf and Stock, 2014

course, were on the paid staff; Natalia was the leader of the movement. Wasn't this how SU had started in 1867? An Australian SU staff member visiting us in England in the 1980s put it succinctly: 'SU is essentially a movement of volunteers, where necessary supported by paid staff.' May that continue to echo through the meeting rooms, offices, conferences and gatherings of SU's leaders, in whichever corner of the globe they are working in today's sophisticated and complex world.

One further visit after retirement, in 2000, took me back to Bratislava – an early spring weekend, meeting up with Natalia, Alena and Vlado, together working the hours of one full-time person. Chris Elston was established in eastern Slovakia, and spending time travelling at weekends, with fruitful opportunities in many churches to preach and introduce SU. Earlier in the year the movement in Slovakia had been able to share in the millennium SU lamp project with an excellent meeting in the Christian school in Bratislava.

Since 2000 I met Natalia on at least two occasions (2010 and 2012) when she was leading the Slovak team participating in the international teen games residential event in Eastern Europe. In 2005 she wrote in one of the bulletins:

SU Slovakia was registered in 1991 and I've been privileged by being able to walk along, experiencing the growth and development of SU ministry here in Slovakia. From the small beginnings, through the first publications and family camps, our ministry has become known in churches, especially among Sunday School Teachers who use our Resource Materials and children and teenagers who have spent several summer camps with us. In our work we use the word 'creativity' very often. We try to teach children in a very creative way, encourage teachers to use new methods and, with limited finances and human resources, we have to be creative and wise. I strongly believe there is no coincidence, that the only memory verse I remember from my own Sunday School days is Psalm 119v105: 'Your word is a lamp to my feet'. This is a strategic verse for SU ministry and is really my motto for life. Appreciating your prayers, Natalia

What of SU in Slovakia today? In one of the recent news bulletins in January 2016, there is a genuine flavour of growth and purposeful activity:

> We have new young leaders in our team, so we do pray for them, we give thanks for their willingness to serve, and we pray that they will be open to hear God s word while we meet regularly in the monthly Bible study group. So they might grow into leaders for SU and churches as well. We will be running a one day holiday club for kids on February 1st. We need to prepare a full day program, and this is first real task for new young volunteers. So we pray for preparation, for kids and leaders as well, so this would be an opportunity to share the Good news with more kids again. We are planning to publish a Bible time line, which is a great teaching aid. Lots of teachers are looking for this, as we are using an English version of a Bible time line in workshops and seminars. We also pray for a Bible study group for teachers, in which Natalia participated, so this will be a blessed place to go deeper into the Bible together.

Bulgaria:
'A Small Land, a Handful of Heaven'

This was Mercia MacDermott's description of Bulgaria in her biography of Vasil Levsky, a nineteenth-century Bulgarian freedom fighter in a conflict against the Turks. Yet this appeared a far cry from the country coming out of the forty years of repressive Marxist rule. From my visit in the autumn of 1992, I had noted that 70% of Bulgarians by tradition are Orthodox, a church that was split, causing open strife (complete with water cannon!) in and around the synod buildings. Protestants (Methodists, Congregationalists, Baptists and Pentecostals) feared strong Orthodox repression once the splits were resolved. One million Turks (11% of the population of Bulgaria) in addition to a considerable number of Pomaks (Bulgarian Muslims)

Helen with Luben Koev displaying the first published teaching materials

Helen visiting Studio 865

First meeting of the Bulgarian SU 'committee' in the early nineties

reflected a substantial minority of Muslims in Bulgaria. Interestingly, there were more Turkish Christians in Bulgaria than in Turkey.

Following my first visit to Bulgaria in April 1991 and over the subsequent weeks of that year, a clear sense of calling to Scripture Union had taken shape in Helen Parry's mind and heart. She had to settle some domestic issues before she was ready to return to Bulgaria in early 1992 as SU's first staff worker there.

Helen was an infinitely adaptable person, who had quickly grasped and, in some charming and amusing ways, had adapted to Bulgarian culture and practice. Each time I visited Bulgaria in subsequent years – and these were many – I could never predict how our programme would shape up. Helen knew, but wisely chose to keep me in the dark – in case of necessary change at the last minute, and perhaps also to spice up my desire to 'live by faith'!

Skilfully and prayerfully, she formed a working committee, which met in the autumn of 1992 at Kazanlak in central Bulgaria. Seven people came to the meeting, from different cities in the central and eastern parts of the country, though none from Sofia. They would work on a draft constitution and they agreed a name: Evangelska Asoziazia Priateli na Bibliata, translated literally into English as 'Evangelical Association of Friends of the Bible'. I felt at the time that 'evangelical' could be misconstrued against the background of Orthodox Church domination in the country.

Yet Helen realised that not all the members of that group had understood the nature and practice of SU ministry, nor were their motives entirely clear. One couple in particular saw SU as a door to resourcing their own plans and projects.

All this led to not a little pain, especially for Helen, who had to withstand misunderstandings and occasional and quite unjustified accusations. She weathered the more adverse circumstances remarkably and, by this time having moved to Sofia, with a base at the Christian Literature Crusade bookshop, she soon 'grew' a network of people on whom she could rely from a variety of church groupings. Kiril Christov, a young man who attended the de Bron SU international conference in the early summer of 1992, was one of these. Over the months, he was to give Helen a great deal of support and assistance. Kiril spoke from the platform one evening at the conference: 'Bulgaria is the doorway of Europe,' he gently declared. 'There are many Turkish Muslims there and some are becoming Christians. I know. I am one of them.'

The destabilising nature of rapid change which I had witnessed in other Eastern European countries was clearly visible in Bulgaria. Restitution (i.e. returning properties to their rightful owners) was proceeding slowly, but with unclear outcomes. New supermarket chains were opening, but with soaring prices, well outside the purchasing power of the average Bulgarian wage earner. Constant and unpredictable changes in the law affected foundations and voluntary associations, including churches and Christian mission agencies. These changes appeared to hamper growth and development.

Following major problems with SU Bulgaria's charitable foundation application, Helen had wisely founded her own 'business'. She named it 'Balkan Traks' and published an English-language tourist guide. And under this banner she directed SU's work and publications for some years, until much later it became possible to register within the law.

Many responsible Bulgarian Christian leaders perceived a danger in the overlap and duplication of much western mission effort. One key leader, at a national initiative forum I attended in September 1992, with forty leaders representing western and Bulgarian missions and leadership of the Bulgarian churches, stated this quite strongly: 'We are disappointed by some missions who are in danger of destroying the work here, in order to realise their programmes ... we are not the jungle, we are not animals ... too much expectation and responsibility is being placed on immature people who have no experience of Christian ministry ... missions can split churches rather than reaching out to the unchurched.' The four main Bulgarian evangelical leaders present supported this statement. It was encouraging that SU appeared to be welcomed in Bulgaria and was regarded as an authentic Christian 'mission'. This was, in no small part, due to the good and faithful work that Helen Parry was pioneering, winning many Bulgarian friends and co-workers.

All the members of the forum were deeply moved when Stoyko Petkov, the leader and founder of the New Christian media group Studio 865, and with whom we were working, stood up to share his testimony in the tragic circumstances of the death of his wife in a road accident only three days earlier. It was a strong reminder of the fragility of life in a hazardous and sometimes chaotic and unpredictable society.

An early venture, in collaboration with 'Mission Possible', a publishing and children's ministry closely linked to the biggest Pentecostal group in Bulgaria, took shape when Scripture Union Bible reading notes were translated from English and inserted into their children's magazine. At the same time, a quiet, gentle man, Luben Koev, who ran a small publishing house 'Vinesong' with his wife Diana, was enthusiastic about the concept of producing SU England's teaching material *Learning Together* in Bulgarian. As in other countries, the plan was to translate and adapt. For several years Luben continued to work with Helen, and help additionally in the key processes of distribution and promotion of this material. Later in the decade, Luben wrote to me of the 'miracle' in the life of his family, in that they had received the coveted green card to settle in the USA. His presence and wisdom seemed a significant loss to the fragile SU movement in Bulgaria. Nevertheless, at the same time God raised others to be involved with SU.

During my visit in 1992, I caught up with Krassi, whom I had first met at the European high schools conference in 1991. Krassi was translating into Bulgarian some English-language resources for Christians in high schools. Helen could use these in training and giving vision to young Christians at school. Richard and Jane Fillingham had recently arrived to work with IFES in the universities. Richard was open to having a high schools volunteer on his team and working closely with Helen.

I scarcely knew Blaga and Ivan when they came to a mountain hostel, near Gabrovo in central Bulgaria, with us for a weekend of praying and planning in the early spring of 1996. I had been introduced briefly to them in the Congregational church in Sofia where they worshipped, but had only exchanged formal greetings on that occasion. Helen had invited a few others including Diana, Luben's wife and faithful in assisting Helen in the production of our early SU Bulgarian printed resources. There were a few others from different churches in Sofia who joined us for that special weekend. I felt this was a significant 'kairos' time for SU in Bulgaria: a prayerful and formative step towards the development and growth of SU in Bulgaria. In her own inimitable way, Helen was able to lead the group through the principles, practices and possibilities of SU for Bulgaria.

I was due to fly home on the following Monday, but a heavy snowfall on the Saturday seemed to put that in doubt. When would we be able to leave the 'mountain fortress' and risk the road twenty miles down the hill to Gabrovo? Helen didn't seem to mind and thought it rather funny. I was not so amused. In the end Sunday morning brought respite in the weather conditions. With great caution, we drove slowly down the slippery, icy mountain road and had time to worship with the local evangelical church, before setting off for Sofia later in the day.

Helen and I could see the potential in Blaga as someone who could take SU forward in Bulgaria. Helen was coming to the end of her contract and felt it was time to make way for Bulgarian leadership of the movement. But she was uncertain as to how Blaga would cope if she were left to hold the SU 'baby' once Helen had gone. I had some misgivings. Blaga was a young woman with a growing family. Her husband was an incredibly busy lawyer, much in demand by churches and new Christian groups struggling to establish their legality in a country where the complex legal system was in a state of constant and chaotic change. Blaga had been working on an occasional basis with Helen in the office, yet Helen was not sure whether Blaga was ready to commit herself to the demands of the growing, untidy and pressured pattern of life that working for SU in Bulgaria would entail.

Helen finally moved back to the UK, towards the end of 1996, after some years of working relentlessly to establish SU Bulgaria and to encourage the small but actively growing committee. Blaga became the leading staff member for SU in Bulgaria, and not only blossomed in the work but was able, with the assistance of her lawyer husband Ivan, to register the movement under the name 'Scripture Union'. She found a new office in an ideal location, and much more suited to SU's requirements. She found Niki, a young student and a computer whizz-kid, who often worked in the office so late that he just slept there and went to his lectures the following morning. Fortunately the office was equipped with a shower.

In the intervening years, SU Bulgaria greatly benefited from the visits of Ruth and Brian Nicholls, Vicki Shaver, Emlyn Williams and David Geddes. Ruth and Brian made two visits: one in 1992, and the following year they stayed for two weeks in the early spring with opportunities for teaching and encouraging children's workers. Vicki Shaver spent three months in the early summer of 1994 staying with Helen in Bankya to encourage and advise. Emlyn and David provided invaluable wisdom in respect of training camp leaders and the opportunities for schools work.

Following a number of visits to Bulgaria over these crucial years from 1990 to 1995, in March 1996 I met Helen for what would be our last meeting before she left for the UK in September of that year. 1996 had seen Helen getting involved in a Roma 'children's church' in one of the deprived and desolate quarters of Sofia; Helen was shocked at the ghetto conditions. Cardboard-patched roofs of the low houses provided little warmth in the long winter. The houses were separated by narrow muddy paths alongside a drain/sewer. Anything between ten and a hundred children attended weekly; ages ranged from one to sixteen!

At the same time, more generally, life was not so straightforward for many believers. Helen told of a respected and experienced school teacher recounting a recent staff meeting when the school director instructed them to inform him of all pupils who attended any of the 'sects' in town (i.e. Protestant churches and other religious groups). Another teacher friend called Helen to say that the State Security (formerly the Secret Police) had visited her to ask whether she knew that a lot of foreign 'sect' members were registering businesses in order to do their work. This legacy from the past repressions had lingered well into the nineties, alongside many other unpredictabilities of life: long queues for petrol and bread; within one short week, the Bulgarian currency (lev) had dropped from 78 to 160 in exchange for one American dollar. Helen had written in November 1994, 'The regime of water in Sofia will be one day off, one day on.'

Yet in the face of these challenging conditions, Helen pioneered a number of teenage camps. A camp at a Black Sea resort for younger teens; an adventure trek in the Rila Mountains; clubs for Roma kids from Sofia and Sliven, and an 'escape to a monastery' for young people from Orthodox and Protestant churches 'who are seriously wanting to share what they have in common'. The publications which Helen had pioneered over these years were greatly valued. 'I am writing to tell you that I very much like "Alone with the Bible". This helps me to read from the Bible for myself, to learn more about Jesus,' wrote ten-year-old Radostina. Petya, a thirteen-year-old, wrote, 'I would like to have every issue; through this God speaks the truth to me.'

One of Helen's goals had been to establish a residential centre in Bulgaria where SU could organise a range of training seminars and evangelistic and discipleship events, with opportunities to host others from SU Europe. This could strengthen the focus on reaching children, young people, families and teams of volunteers essential to strong growth of any SU movement. As early as September 1992 Helen had given some serious thought to this, and had begun to explore possible sites.

Bansko was a delightful and attractive tourist centre in southern Bulgaria, on the edge of the Pirin Mountains. Today it is a much-visited European ski resort. Even in the early nineties we felt it had many of the elements that would attract people to attend SU activities. Helen had written to the town mayor explaining who we were and what we were looking for. Following a two-and-a-half-hour journey from Sofia, we met with one of his officials who explained politely that in this period of national restitution, not many people were ready or willing to sell their newly acquired lands or property. There was a possibility of leasing a property from friends of SU. We viewed it and came to the conclusion that it might have possibilities. Yet the building was incomplete; why not ask the owners to reflect on this and let us know how they felt? They were members of the local Congregational church and seemed sympathetic to our goals. Yet there were complications, and family interests.

Over the next few years, Helen continued to explore other possibilities. Another property had been returned to a Christian family who had owned the land in the pre-communist era. It was a two-storey house with eight rooms and a yard! There was still uncertainty, politically and economically. Moreover the ownership of the land was being disputed. In all these possibilities we needed, above all, to discern what God's will was.

My overall concern about purchasing property in any of the newly 'freed' countries was that, while I had seen and valued residential sites in the developed SU movements in the west, it seemed that there were significant risks for the new and often fragile SU movements. Commitment to the upkeep and regular use of real estate would make financial demands that would not be easy. At this stage, committed people were the first priority, and spending scarce financial resources on a building at this stage might not be the wisest policy. The project in Croatia was perhaps an exception and today has proved its value in the longer term.

From 1997, Blaga built on the foundations established earlier by Helen and the faithful volunteers. She began to develop all kinds of exciting ventures. She soon began to build networks with IFES, the Association of Christian Teachers, and Tentmakers International – just to mention a few. She made deals with bookshops and publishers and in the following eight years took SU many steps forward. A solid and supportive committee has been formed, ably chaired by Ventsi Stoikov, a young man with a good track record in working with local churches and with a sensitive and wise character.

My wife Valerie and I visited Bulgaria in the early spring of 2000. Blaga arranged for us to stay in a flat belonging to the mother of the SU chairman. It was in a typical communist ten-storey faceless block, with a lift without a door. We were on the tenth floor. From the living-room window we looked down on a marauding tribe of dogs prowling the adjacent waste land. Each morning Blaga sent a car to collect us, so that we did not have to weave our way through the assortment of animals! Inside the flat we had a comfortable bed, a kitchen with a fridge – what more did we need? By the end of the week we had discovered that the fridge froze the milk; we subsequently poured juice on our cereal; two days later we found the juice had frozen, so we poured cold tea on our cereal!

No longer based at the CLC bookshop, but sited in an excellent position in the centre of Sofia, the SU office was always a hive of activity. Many people coming and going including Nicki Zlatev, one of whose duties was to collect Sveta, Blaga's youngest daughter, from playgroup each day. Yet he put in more than forty hours a week in the office, mainly with the computer and dealing with the administration against a background of complex and ever-changing laws. With committees and meetings going on in the SU office, Valerie took herself off to explore central Sofia or to go out with Radi and Buba, Blaga's teenage daughters, jumping on and off the rattling tram cars, in search of cakes for celebrations later that day. I wrote in my notes:

> I was very encouraged, believing that SU Bulgaria, although a small movement, is in good shape ... it is amazing that Blaga is able to do as much as she does, and given her family responsibilities – yet there is a need for more than one staff worker – could we raise additional funding from a circle of supporting churches in the UK? – my target would be $750 – for a full time appointment they would need $1800 per annum.

Beyond all that we noted a still profoundly unstable economy. No
social benefits had been paid in one big provincial town since
August 1999, because there were no central government grants
available. There had been significant changes in the 'religious laws'
– it seemed like they were going backwards to the situation in 1949.
Yet wonderfully, in the face of all the social and constitutional chaos,
SU Bulgaria were planning four camps in the summer: one
children's, two teenagers', and a family camp at which Daniel
Poujol, national leader of SU France, would speak. Moreover there
was a very effective and committed group of supporters, from a
wide range of churches, who were informally meeting the first
'seeds' of the SU Bulgaria committee.

My last visit to Bulgaria was in 2010 when I was spending
nineteen days in Eastern Europe. Having caught a flight from
Budapest on a Sunday afternoon in mid-July, I was met at a now
much modernised Sofia airport terminal and, after a quick meal, we
travelled to the site of the planned teen games event (with more
than a hundred young people from Serbia, Slovakia, Poland and

International high school students at Teen Games 2010

Bulgaria, in addition to an international team of leaders). The Polish contingent had arrived by bus! The site had been chosen because of the excellent facilities for sports (football, athletics, volleyball, table tennis). However, it had seen better days. It was an extensive set of buildings on different levels, built originally by one of the early communist leaders of Bulgaria as his country retreat; it had over the years been grossly neglected, yet provided sufficient accommodation for us, plus at least two other groups of Bulgarian children.

We began well with presentations from the countries, planned Bible studies and plenary meetings. The food was quite basic and the sleeping accommodation even more so. But things seemed to be running smoothly by Monday evening.

Tuesday morning started well with a good presentation and worship, then to the various games and tournament rounds. But some of the leaders were called to a hastily assembled meeting. In the next few minutes we were told to move out of our rooms and assemble down in the courtyard. The authorities were closing the site – for good, and with immediate notice. It was declared a health hazard as several children in the other groups had become ill and one or two were in hospital.

Blaga, who was now the chairperson of the Bulgarian SU, acted immediately with immense skill and foresight. Within a couple of hours most of our group were on our way to Bansko – the tourist resort in southern Bulgaria where I had travelled some years before with Helen and others. We were accommodated in a four-star hotel! The living conditions were a transformation. The facilities for a full-blown sports programme were not quite so sophisticated, so 'improvisation' was the name of the game. The hotel had no running track, so athletics were organised – running round the perimeter of the hotel complex did us just fine. There was quite a lot of 'hanging out' – some of the sports couldn't be sustained. Other 'novel' sports were invented. Competition was fierce. Chris, the Polish leader, had to intervene when there was a diplomatic incident between the Serb and Bulgarian students and leaders, who had a sharp disagreement about the rules of the relay race. But overall and with at least two off-site excursions, the week was successful. Sharing, worship, teaching, national presentations in the morning and evening were lively and innovative.

A contemporary flavour of SU Bulgaria is reflected in their 2015 news bulletin:

We're having our annual ski camp (31 January – 3 February), which is a great opportunity to meet non-Christians in an informal environment. Please pray for nice weather, snow and for the people who are going. In March we're having 2 big events – the Bible competitions for teens and for students – on 12 March and 26 March, respectively. Please pray for their preparation, so that everyone can have a great time with the Bible. Pray for the different teams, their coaches, the jury, who are thinking up many different questions from the Bible, for all the staff, who are working behind scenes to make it happen. We don't have a specific date for the beginning yet, but we do have enthusiastic volunteers for the idea 'Team on Wheels'. This mobile team will travel around the country, visit small towns and churches and help there with teambuilding games, giving materials for Sunday school teachers and advertising SU Bulgaria to them, so that they know who we are and how we can be of help to them.

Kosovo:
A Late Addition to SU Europe

—— ☙ ——

The state of Yugoslavia was created at the end of World War I. Kosovo, before this date, was part of Albania; today, Albanians make up the majority of the population of Kosovo and around 93% of the people of present-day Kosovo, a 'secular' state, are (at least nominally) Muslim. The war with Serbia (1998–1999) was an ugly and devastating part of the drastic changes which took place in the 'dismantling' of the former Yugoslavia. Many homes were destroyed and more than 13,000 Kosovars were killed. Some estimates claim more than 1 million Kosovars were expatriated forcibly to one of the three neighbouring countries. Families faced displacement, brutality and slaughter. NATO and the USA intervened and Kosovo, now under the protection of the UN, is recognised as a sovereign state.

Since 2009 Brian and BLynn Bowen have been living in Kosovo, where Brian began work at the American University. Earlier in his career, Brian had been in Africa where he had met Bill Roberts, formerly a member of the SU staff in Nigeria and Sierra Leone, living now in the village of Bunessan on the southern tip of the Isle of Mull.

Brian had caught an infectious enthusiasm for Scripture Union while working in Sierra Leone and in 2011 Bill asked Brian whether Scripture Union existed in Kosovo. Bill, curious, directed Brian to me, and Brian and BLynn visited me one evening in Watford in June 2011 on their way to catch a flight. Subsequently we had some exchanges of emails and met up just outside Bicester in June 2012. Later, in October that year, I travelled to Kosovo to meet some friends of Brian and BLynn, most of whom were former Muslims, leading small but growing congregations. It was a short weekend visit, Thursday evening through to Monday morning; even shorter than expected for me as I became ill on Saturday night and spent Sunday in bed. My hosts were Kujtim and Gezime, a young couple who lovingly looked after me and eventually took me to the American hospital for a check-over. Nothing more serious than a touch of food poisoning was diagnosed, and I was able to limp back to the UK the following day, passing the Bill Clinton statue in Pristina en route to the airport.

Earlier, I had spent some time meeting Christians on Friday, and on the following day we had a bumpy two-hour journey to Kamenicë, a small town in eastern Kosovo, where a new church plant was celebrating its opening. Prior to the meeting to open the new church, we sat in a local restaurant with a number of the believers, where there was real and genuine interest, I sensed, in how SU might develop as a movement in Kosovo. The priority seemed to be Bible-related resources for helping the Christian community to engage with God's word, and exploring ways of working with teenagers against the background of sensitivity within a predominantly (even if nominally) Muslim community.

Before I returned to England, I proposed that they consider translating and publishing either the E100 (one hundred 'essential' readings from the Old and New Testament with short explanations on each passage) or preferably *The Essential Jesus* (one hundred readings from the Bible with comments on the person and work of Christ). The young man with whom I had stayed over the weekend was ready to do some translation.

I subsequently contacted the SU European Region to discover that there was a possible plan to publish the E100 in Albanian through a combined initiative in Central Europe and in co-operation with the Bible Societies from five or six of these countries. So it seemed sensible to move ahead with *The Essential Jesus*. Kujtim began the translation work and we found some initial funding for this. There was a Christian publishing house in Pristina and I had spoken during my short visit to the director, who was willing to take this on.

Initial reaction to beginning a new SU movement in Kosovo was cautious. The European Region some time before had taken the general decision not to start new movements in Europe for the time being. In January 2012 the regional director, Monika Kuschmierz, visited Kosovo and saw the potential for SU there. A committee was formed, chaired by Brian, and they found a young man, Gramos Hoxha, who was ready to give time to SU in exploring work with teenagers through sport. In March 2013 the SU Europe council formally recognised the formation of SU Kosova.

Pastor Hilki Berisha, a dentist by profession and working in a church plant in the small town of Kamenicë, showed enthusiasm for the potential of SU work in his country. Hilki and his wife Denida travelled to the UK in the autumn of 2014. At pretty short notice we scrambled an itinerary which offered them exposure to the different flavours of SU in England and Scotland. As Hilki wrote, following the visit:

> With the SU community in UK we had an opportunity to share the SU Kosova story, to share about Kosovo, as well as meet staff in a number of SU offices and hear about their work; participate in some schools programs, attend a prayer meeting for Scripture Union; and hearing about outreach to mixed cultural communities. We have gained such excellent impressions of the people working with SU. Their personal lives were an encouragement; the fact that working for SU was not only working for an organization but was a way of life, living for Christ.

Meanwhile Gramos Hoxha, who has been studying at university, continued to develop a sports ministry through football tournaments and subsequently football camps around Kosovo. He and Brian have also been spending time visiting pastors in seeking to introduce SU in the churches. In July 2016, Gramos will marry and then move to Sweden.

At the beginning of March 2016, Pastor Driton Krasniqi began as the first SU national leader. Brian Bowen wrote:

We are thankful to God that Pastor Driton, with all his skills and experience, has accepted this appointment to serve with SU and further establish the SU Ministry in Kosovo. SU Kosova is the first SU national movement in the Albanian speaking world and the 27th European national movement. Please also kindly pray with us for the March 28th SU Football Tournament (Easter Monday in Prishtina) and for the April 25-27 Youth Camp, proposed for Peje. At the March 11-12 KPEC Assembly we will be distributing copies of the recently published Albanian version of the ESSENTIAL JESUS daily devotional (a partnership project between SU and 'Tenda' Publishing House). Two other SU publications, a Bible daily devotional on the Letter to the Ephesians and also our first children's book 'My Little Blue Book' will become available this spring. Pray that these projects will be useful to God's Kingdom and for Pastor Driton as he starts his first year as SU National Leader while also serving his final year as the KPEC President ... Pray for the future law on religion and religious communities.

First SU Kosova football tournament opens with a prayer in Pristina,
December 2014

The SU Kosova Board, December 2015

Esenca Jezus, January 2016

Daily devotional on the Gospel of Mark, written and produced 100% in Kosovo in 2015. The theme: 'Shpresë për ty' ('hope for you')

Epilogue

—— ๑ ๑ ——

Twenty-five years ago, in 1991, there was a simple yet touching gathering in the heart of London. At the Scripture Union national office, some friends of SU met with former staff along with David Cohen, Peter Chapman, Michael Bewes, Lyn Simmons and Hilary Guest, to dedicate a beautiful table. The table had been crafted and gifted by Graham Laird, as a tribute to his parents, John and Marion Laird. John had led the SU movement in England and Wales in the immediate post-war era, and had helped shape the remarkable growth of SU over that period and beyond for more than twenty years.

Peter and Lyn Chapman wrote:

> Graham was a highly skilled craftsman, and there was some delightful thinking behind the overall design. It was a round table, so that no-one was at the head. Its design did not depict something inherently hierarchical [this was clearly very important to Graham and to David Cohen, then SU's general director, who had discussed the details and suggested the shape]. Graham had made an accompanying wooden plaque, providing a key to all the woods used. As it was being fashioned in his workshop he must have had deep memories going through his mind about his parents and SU and its international reach. It was a delightful table to work at, and we had many meetings around it in David [Cohen]'s office. It was made out of a range of woods, thoughtfully chosen, and sourced from various overseas countries, depicting SU International.

The table, which is still in the Scripture Union office at Milton Keynes, is surely a reflection of the strength, blend and diversity of the global family of Scripture Union.

At the de Bron international conference in 1992, Paul Clark, regional secretary of SU in the Americas, said, memorably, 'Scripture Union today has a dark face, blond hair, wears a kimono, and speaks Spanish.' At the same conference, Alan Martin, the former general director of SU England and Wales, who had been a great encourager to me over the eighties in helping me to understand and respond to God's calling to work in Central and Eastern Europe, said, 'We are all learners, we need each other and we must share talents.'

These words and the experience of being part of SU since the late 1940s taught me to be wary of hierarchies, and shaped and sharpened my aim of helping the new SU movements in Eastern Europe to develop and flourish, to encourage 'communities of purpose' growing servant leaders and committed teams of volunteers. I am mindful of mistakes and misjudgements that I made; was I too impatient to analyse a situation properly before jumping to conclusions and sometimes taking decisions that backfired? On the other hand, was I sometimes too slow to seize opportunities for holy risk-taking, thus losing momentum in planning for growth? Reassuringly, there were others who stepped out and dared to risk; who waited for God's 'kairos' time and then moved 'in step with the Spirit'. Ultimately, as Paul writes in the third chapter of his first letter to the Corinthians, 'Neither the one who plants nor the one who waters is anything, but only God who makes things grow … we are God's fellow workers.'